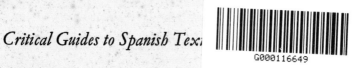

Critical Guides to Spanish Text

EDITED BY J. E. VAREY AND A. D.

Critical Guides to Spanish Texts

8   Antonio Machado : Campos de Castilla

ANTONIO MACHADO

Campos de Castilla

Arthur Terry
Professor of Literature, University of Essex

Grant & Cutler Ltd *in association with*
Tamesis Books Ltd 1973

© Grant & Cutler Ltd
1973
ISBN 0 900411 63 5
Printed in England at
The Compton Press Ltd
for
GRANT & CUTLER LTD
11 BUCKINGHAM STREET, LONDON, W.C.2.

Contents

References

In all recent editions of Machado's *Poesías completas*, the individual poems are printed and numbered in the same order. Several of these editions, including that published in the Austral series (Espasa-Calpe, Madrid), also contain Machado's own prefaces and the prose version of "La tierra de Alvargonzález". A good deal of Machado's other prose, including most of the passages I have quoted, is easily accessible in the excellent four-volume anthology edited by Aurora de Albornoz (see Bibliographical Note).

The figures in brackets in italic type refer to the numbered items in the Bibliographical Note; the italic figure is followed by a page reference.

For Charles Tomlinson and Henry Gifford

1 Introduction

Campos de Castilla was first published in 1912, when Machado was thirty-six. Later, in the *Poesías completas* of 1917, he added about sixty poems, and it is this fuller version which appears in all subsequent editions.* These bare facts conceal a moving and tragic personal history which deeply affects what, for many readers, is Machado's greatest poetic achievement. Nevertheless, it is easy to oversimplify: though *Campos de Castilla* contains a high proportion of Machado's best poems, it would be wrong to praise these at the expense of his earlier volume, *Soledades, galerías y otros poemas* (1907), just as it is a mistake to assume – as is sometimes done – that his talent for poetry had exhausted itself by 1917.

What marks off *Campos de Castilla* from Machado's earlier work is partly a matter of circumstances. As he put it himself in his preface to the *Páginas escogidas* of 1917:

> Cinco años en la tierra de Soria, hoy para mí sagrada – allí me casé, allí perdí a mi esposa, a quien adoraba –, orientaron mis ojos y mi corazón hacia lo esencial castellano . . .;

in other words, a new personal relationship and a new landscape, which he was also to explore in specifically human terms. This interplay between the personal and the collective – between his own inner life and the wish to communicate on a more universal level – was to occupy Machado in various forms for the rest of his life. The interesting thing, as far as *Campos de Castilla* is concerned, is the extent to which the poems embody certain aims which Machado had already formulated, in theory at least, before 1907.

Machado's first collection of poems, *Soledades*, is dated 1903. As he later confessed, "la ideología dominante era eminentemente subjetivista", a kind of subjectivity which, in his case, owed a

*For a list of the poems contained in the 1912 edition of *Campos de Castilla,* see Appendix.

great deal to the examples of other poets, notably Rubén Darío
and Verlaine. At the time Machado began to write, the influence
of Darío – "el maestro incomparable de la forma y de la sen-
sación" – was inescapable. Looking back on this early phase in
1917, Machado writes as though he had been simultaneously
attracted and repelled by the work of the older poet. What is
clear from his remarks is that Darío at this stage stood for an
ideal of aesthetic refinement which tended to neglect the true
sources of the imagination :

> Pensaba yo que el elemento poético no era la palabra por su
> valor fónico, ni el color, ni la línea, ni un complejo de sen-
> saciones, sino una honda palpitación del espíritu . . .

Here, the implied criticism of Darío, and of *modernismo* in
general, is accurate enough. At the same time, Machado is speaking with hindsight, and in doing so, concealing something of the
conflict which he clearly experienced at this early point in his
work.

Part of the evidence for this lies in the differences between the
original edition of *Soledades* and the revised version – *Soledades,
galerías y otros poemas* – of 1907. As Dámaso Alonso has shown,
Machado excluded a number of the more obviously *modernista*
poems from the later edition, thereby giving a greater unity to
the collection as a whole.* This is not to say that the *modernista*
influence disappears entirely : it continues to appear, not only
in a number of the poems Machado preserved, like "Horizonte"
[XVII] and "Abril florecía . . ." [XXXVIII], but also, as we
shall see, at certain moments in *Campos de Castilla*. Nor does
he completely reject the symbols of the park and the formal gar-
den which he had inherited from Verlaine, or the vague feminine
visions ("algún vagar de túnica ligera") which appear even in a
poem as accomplished as "El limonero lánguido suspende . . ."
[VII].

This last poem, not included in *Soledades*, though published
for the first time in 1903, shows how difficult it is to draw the
line chronologically between the two collections. Some of the

---

*"Poesías olvidadas de Antonio Machado", in *Poetas españoles contem-
poráneos* (Madrid, 1952), 103–59.

most impressive and characteristic poems of the later book were written only a matter of months after the completion of *Soledades* in 1902. Many of these slightly later poems are prefigured in one of the best poems from *Soledades* :

> Sobre la tierra amarga
> caminos tiene el sueño
> laberínticos, sendas tortuosas,
> parques en flor y en sombra y en silencio;
>
> criptas hondas, escalas sobre estrellas;
> retablos de esperanzas y recuerdos.
> Figurillas que pasan y sonríen
> — juguetes melancólicos de viejo –;
>
> imágenes amigas,
> a la vuelta florida del sendero,
> y quimeras rosadas
> que hacen camino . . . lejos . . .
>
> [XXII]*

Here, the first two lines neatly bridge the gap between dream and reality : because of his confidence in the inner vision, we might say, Machado realizes its power to impinge on the world and to transform the objects and situations he encounters on his mental journey. At the same time, there is a sense of isolation : the "figurillas que pasan y sonríen" appear to exist at one remove from the speaker, even before the more obvious distancing which takes place in the last two lines. This mood of loneliness partly, though not entirely, explains the melancholy which, as often in Machado's early poems, seems to suggest a feeling of premature age : the awareness, so beautifully caught in "Crear fiestas de amores . . ." [XXVIII], of having failed to achieve some central, but indefinable, experience.

Nevertheless, in spite of many uncertainties, what Machado has understood by this stage is that any sense of his own identity is inseparable from the twin functions of dream and memory. In "El limonero lánguido suspende . . .", he has returned to the

---

*In the original edition of *Soledades*, line 9 reads "imágenes *sombrías*". This was revised in 1907; as Geoffrey Ribbans points out: "Con el cambio de una sola palabra, Machado ha desechado la agria melancolía de su primera actitud para reconciliarse plenamente con las visiones por él ideadas" (*12*, 168).

patio of the house in Seville where he spent his early childhood :

> y estoy solo, en el patio silencioso,
> buscando una ilusión cándida y vieja : . . .

This "illusion" centres on the image of the fruits reflected in the water of the fountain : these reflected fruits, he remembers, were part of the magic of childhood – once, as a child, he had tried to grasp them, as if they were the clue to a deeper reality – and the memory of the earlier situation brings with it the possibility of hope. This hope is irrational and uncertain :

> En el ambiente de la tarde flota
> ese aroma de ausencia
> que dice al alma luminosa : nunca,
> y al corazón : espera.

By the end of the poem, the magic has been transferred to the present ("los frutos encantados/que hoy en el fondo de la fuente sueñan . . ."). Looking back over the process which has led up to this, we see that the importance of the memory for Machado lies in its persistence; what he has recaptured is not merely a moment in his childhood, but a guarantee of the truth of his present vision. At the same time, the total effect of the poem is more subtle than this. In contrasting the tired appearance of the lemon-tree ("El limonero lánguido suspende/una pálida rama polvo-rienta . . .") with the freshness of the reflected fruits, it is as if Machado were trying to establish the distance between his normal state of mind and the glimpse of a hidden reality which exists, not in the observed details of the scene, but within his own consciousness. Thus a great deal in the poem depends on the balance it maintains between the registering of particular detail and the way in which these same details act as metaphors for the speaker's emotions. The gradual process of exploration which this involves is a permanent characteristic of Machado's best poetry, just as the interplay between reality and meditation is a vital part of his treatment of landscape in *Campos de Castilla*. As for the relations between dream and memory, one begins to see, even at this early stage, how the latter, for Machado, is much more than a simple act of recollection. As Zubiría observes : "Machado, más que recordar sus recuerdos, lo que hacía era soñarlos" (*15*, 68);

that is to say, memory, if it is to be really meaningful, must become part of the deeper vision which is the true source of his poetry. Or, as he himself put it, in one of the most moving poems of the later collection :

> mas falta el hilo que el recuerdo anuda
> al corazón, el ancla en su ribera,
> o estas memorias no son alma . . .
> [CXXV]

In *Soledades, galerías y otros poemas* (1907), the fusion of dream and memory is achieved through the central symbol of the *galerías del alma*. At their most obvious level, the *Galerías* poems present a more inward version of the "journeying" theme which appears in *Soledades* : the landscape through which the poet moves is no longer an external one, but the imaginary labyrinth of his own consciousness, a network of "galleries" presided over by certain guiding spirits. In his introductory poem [LXI], Machado clearly asserts the visionary nature of the poet :

> El alma del poeta
> se orienta hacia el misterio.
> Sólo el poeta puede
> mirar lo que está lejos
> dentro del alma, en turbio
> y mago sol envuelto.

Here, the magical quality of the shifting light suggests both the precariousness of the vision and its inevitability. Significantly, Machado refers to the "galerías . . . del *recuerdo*", implying that it is the poet alone who can come to terms with the workings of memory and bring them into the present. As the poem goes on, the rift which separates the poet from other men is widened :

> El alma que no sueña,
> el enemigo espejo,
> proyecta nuestra imagen
> con un perfil grotesco.

To deny the imagination, therefore, is to look into a distorting mirror, and this seems deliberately contrasted with the very different kind of mirror – the "profundo/espejo de mis sueños" –

with which the poem opens. It is the truthful "mirror" of the imagination which enables the poet to turn his memories into the materials of the future ("la nueva miel labramos/con los dolores viejos"), and so to imitate the activity of dreams themselves, the "laborar eterno/. . . de las doradas/abejas de los sueños".

In lines like these, Machado is clearly drawing on the richness and possible ambiguity of the word *sueño* : the mental states he is attempting to describe are not so much "dreams" in the normal sense as "waking dreams", in which fantasy projects its own truths on the actual experiences of the past. The best of the *Galerías* poems, like those which follow the introduction [LXII–IV], seem to come from a world of the imagination which has almost broken its links with observed reality. Almost, but not entirely : details like those in the first of these pieces – ". . . ¡El limonar florido,/el cipresal del huerto . . .!" – have already appeared in earlier, more descriptive poems. The difference now is that they have become part of a momentary vision : fragmentary images of the past, to be grasped at before they fade. Inevitably, the moods which they help to create are unstable and hard to define : as Ribbans has pointed out (*12*, 200), Machado's attitude in these poems – and in many others – tends to oscillate between despair and temporary hope. What is at stake is not only his sense of the hidden meaning of life, but also his belief in the genuineness of his own poetic talent. And however much these attitudes continue to affect his later poems, it seems true to say that he was never again to be introspective in quite this way, or with such persistence.

It is interesting that Machado himself seems to have realized at a surprisingly early stage the difficulty of proceeding further in this direction. Some of the most striking of the *Galerías* poems, including the three just mentioned, were first published in 1903–04. In 1903, Machado wrote to Miguel de Unamuno : "Empiezo a creer . . . que el artista debe amar la vida y odiar el arte." Taken in isolation, this may seem no more than a reaction against the more artificial side of *modernismo*. However, in another letter to Unamuno, written in the following year, Machado is more explicit :

No debemos crearnos un mundo aparte en que gozar fantástica y egoístamente la contemplación de nosotros mismos: no debemos huir de la vida para forjarnos una vida mejor que sea estéril para los demás . . . La belleza no está en el misterio sino en el deseo de penetrarlo. Pero este camino es muy peligroso y puede llevarnos a hacer un caos en nosotros mismos si no caemos en la vanidad de crear sistemáticamente temas que, en realidad, no existen, no deben existir (quoted 7, 26).

Here, the note of self-criticism is unmistakable. In his letters and other writings of the time, Machado freely acknowledges the part played by Unamuno in suggesting the possibility of a less self-absorbed kind of poetry. As we shall see, this is not the only period at which Unamuno exercised a decisive influence on Machado, though one should not underestimate Machado's own awareness of the problems which confronted him as a poet.

These seem to have been particularly acute in the months following the publication of *Soledades*. In a letter written about February, 1904, he confessed to his younger contemporary Juan Ramón Jiménez:

No estoy muy satisfecho de las cosas que hago últimamente. Estoy en un período de evolución y todavía no he encontrado forma de expresión de mi nueva poesía (quoted *12, 209*).

Like Machado, Jiménez had begun to write verse under the influence of Darío, Verlaine and certain minor French symbolists, as well as sharing an admiration for the nineteenth-century Andalusian poet Gustavo Adolfo Bécquer. A month or so after the letter I have just quoted, Machado published a review of Jiménez's most recent collection of poems, *Arias tristes*. Though he is deeply sympathetic towards the book (it is, after all, not long since he himself was trying to write a similar kind of poetry), Machado is not uncritical. At one point he says:

Tristeza o alegría, ¿qué son al fin sino esas mismas sensaciones [i.e. the sensations which form the basis of Jiménez's poems] fundidas y acrisoladas al contraste de nuestra luz interna, más o menos turbia, y expresadas en una voz propia que dice: vivimos hacia la vida o hacia la muerte? Juan R. Jiménez se ha dedicado a soñar, apenas ha vivido vida activa, vida real.

And at another:

> ... yo no puedo aceptar que el poeta sea un hombre estéril que
> huya de la vida para forjarse quiméricamente una vida mejor
> en que gozar de la contemplación de sí mismo. Y he añadido
> ¿no seríamos capaces de soñar con los ojos abiertos en la vida
> activa, en la vida militante? (4, II, 87–9).

In the first passage, Machado is not so much denying the
validity of the other poet's sensations, as suggesting their lack of
genuine emotion: true sadness or happiness, he argues, are only
possible if one's sensations are weighed in the perspective of
life and death. The second statement applies equally well to
Machado's own early work, and the final sentence is echoed in a
striking poem [LX], published for the first time in 1907. Here,
the opening question – "¿Mi corazón se ha dormido?" – returns
to the fear of poetic sterility which occurs in several of the
Galerías poems. The second stanza, however, is quite unequivo-
cal:

> No, mi corazón no duerme.
> Está despierto, despierto.
> Ni duerme ni sueña, mira,
> los claros ojos abiertos,
> señas lejanas y escucha
> a orillas del gran silencio.

Like other poems of Machado's, this has the effect both of
summarizing a whole process of feeling and of marking out fresh
territory to be explored. It would be an oversimplification to say
that Machado had abandoned a subjective mode of poetry in
favour of a more objective one. "Subjectivity" and "objectivity"
are never very precise terms, and in a poet like Machado a great
deal depends on the balance between the writer's own sensibility
and his awareness of his own situation in space and time. In the
lines I have just quoted, the sense of mystery is as great as ever,
but now it depends on looking outward, on attending to the
"signs" and the "silence" which are present in the world itself.

The process which leads to this awareness is a long one, and
this alone should warn us against making too sharp a distinction
between *Campos de Castilla* and the earlier poems. The strengths

of *Campos de Castilla* cannot be explained merely by the change in Machado's personal circumstances, however vital this may have been. It is perhaps truer to say that Machado's understanding of these circumstances could hardly have taken the form it did without the kind of attitudes we have just seen. As Ribbans has said :

> El cambio de orientación de Antonio Machado que procede de la crisis que postulamos hacia 1904 produce una nueva y creciente tendencia a ocuparse de asuntos y objetos externos, si bien éstos siguen estando estrechamente relacionados con su vida y sus emociones. Forma parte de este nuevo rumbo lo que podríamos llamar el respeto a la identidad de las cosas, la conciencia de su existencia objetiva e independiente, cualesquiera que sean las asociaciones que nosotros les imponemos (*12*, 227).

The essential shift is here, if it is anywhere. The question of the relations between the creating self and the external world was to occupy Machado for the rest of his life, and in the end it took him further than he could have conceived at the time of *Campos de Castilla*. Whatever form it assumes, the fact that such a problem lies at the centre of Machado's work means that he is an essentially Romantic artist, and one of exceptional lucidity and intelligence. In much of the most interesting nineteenth-century poetry, there is an attempt to reconcile the claims of the individual sensibility and those of a world which, at the worst, may seem hostile and unrelated. There is good reason to suppose that Machado would have endorsed Baudelaire's famous statement :

> [The modern concept of art] is to create a suggestive magic including at the same time object and subject, the world outside the artist and the artist himself.

At times, *Campos de Castilla* has a "magic" of its own, which is quite unlike the consciously invited magic of the *Galerías* poems. What is crucial, however, is the new respect for the "identity of things" : not, as Machado was to learn, an infallible means to objectivity, but a fresh challenge to the perceiving eye and to the reflective sensibility already so remarkably evident in the earlier poems.

1. The sense of a landscape

In April, 1907, a few months before the publication of *Soledades, galerías y otros poemas*, Machado was appointed Professor of French at the Instituto de Segunda Enseñanza in Soria. He visited Soria for three days at the beginning of May, and finally took up his post in September of the same year. The earliest of his Soria poems dates, in fact, from this first brief visit, and was completed in time to be included in his forthcoming collection :

ORILLAS DEL DUERO
Se ha asomado una cigüeña a lo alto del campanario.
Girando en torno a la torre y al caserón solitario,
ya las golondrinas chillan. Pasaron del blanco invierno
de nevascas y ventiscos los crudos soplos de infierno.
    Es una tibia mañana.
El sol calienta un poquito la pobre tierra soriana.

Pasados los verdes pinos,
casi azules, primavera
se ve brotar en los finos
chopos de la carretera
y del río. El Duero corre, terso y mudo, mansamente.
El campo parece, más que joven, adolescente.

Entre las hierbas alguna humilde flor ha nacido,
azul o blanca. ¡Belleza del campo apenas florido,
y mística primavera !

¡Chopos del camino blanco, álamos de la ribera,
espuma de la montaña
ante la azul lejanía,
sol del día, claro día !
¡Hermosa tierra de España !

[IX]

In many ways, this reads like a sketch for the more elaborate poems of *Campos de Castilla*. The way in which it builds up from bare factual observation to the more emotional pitch of the final exclamations; the careful interplay of tenses ("Se ha asomado . . ."; "ya . . . chillan"; "Pasaron . . ."; "Es una tibia mañana"); the accurate registering of colours ("verdes, . . . casi azules") : all these are characteristics which appear again and again in Machado's later poems. One notices also the transition from "objective" description to the implied presence of the spectator ("se ve brotar . . ."; "El campo parece . . ."), which at least suggests how the observed landscape may become part of a deeper mental process. The effect of the ending is slightly more complex; the emotional charge is directed partly through the elements of the landscape, arranged in a sequence which moves from the foreground to the distance, and partly through more sweeping gestures: "¡Belleza del campo . . . ,/y mística primavera!" and "¡Hermosa tierra de España!" What saves the last phrase from banality is a sense of hidden implications: a surprised recognition that what has just been described is the concentrated essence of a larger whole – not merely "Spain", but a particular set of feelings about Spain. What those feelings might be is only hinted at in the rest of the poem; yet the effect of earlier phrases like "la pobre tierra soriana", "alguna humilde flor" and "campo apenas florido" is to suggest a feeling of wonder, and perhaps also of melancholy, at the emergence of natural beauty in a bleak and unpromising setting.

If the later Soria poems are more complex than this, it is not only because of Machado's increasing powers of observation and understanding, but also because his thoughts come to centre more and more on what it means to be living in a particular place at a particular time. In this, of course, Machado was not alone : other contemporary writers, notably Unamuno and Azorín, had already created an image of Castile which was part of the wider reassessment of Spanish values and culture which was gathering weight at the end of the nineteenth century. A great deal has been written about the so-called "Generation of 1898" and the general mood of disillusionment which was crystallized by the loss of Cuba, the last of the Spanish colonies in the New World. In one way or another, the failure of moral confidence, brought on by a long process of corruption in public life, can be seen in every important writer of the time. What makes it possible to speak of a "generation" is not so much a question of chronology (Unamuno, for instance, was nine years older than Machado) as of the existence of a common sensibility : the awareness of a particular crisis of integrity and the search for a means of regeneration at both the individual and social levels. Machado's own view of his relationship to the other members of the generation is a little ambiguous. In an interview given in 1938, he declared :

> Soy posterior a ella [i.e. the 1898 generation]. Mi relación con aquellos hombres – Unamuno, Baroja, Ortega, Valle-Inclán – es la de un discípulo con sus maestros. Cuando yo nacía a la vida literaria y filosófica, todos aquellos hombres eran ya valores cuajados y en sazón (quoted *14*, 34).

The omission of Azorín, with whom he has more in common than with Baroja, and the inclusion of Ortega y Gasset, his junior by eight years, are curious. Nevertheless, it seems certain that, in writing the poems of *Campos de Castilla*, Machado was both synthesizing a great deal of what had already been expressed in a more scattered form by other members of the generation and suggesting a different kind of relationship between the past and the future.

Machado shares with Unamuno a sense of the central importance of Castile in the moulding of Spanish traditions, and both are haunted by a landscape whose present poverty is overshadowed by the memory of past greatness. This contrast, often painful in its intensity, goes with an awareness of certain permanent qualities – austerity, dignity, and at times cruelty – which have survived the fluctuations of history. In one of his most influential books, *En torno al casticismo* (1895), Unamuno explores the concept of *intrahistoria*, the idea that the most significant part of a nation's life takes place beneath the surface of historical events :

> Esa vida intra-histórica, silenciosa y continua como el fondo mismo del mar, es la sustancia misma del progreso, la verdadera tradición eterna, no la tradición mentida que se suele ir a buscar al pasado enterrado en libros y papeles y monumentos y piedras.*

*Obras completas, 16 vols. (Madrid, 1959–64), III, 185.

There is no doubt that Machado accepted Unamuno's version of the conflict between *historia* and *intrahistoria*, and that this helps to explain the almost Wordsworthian compassion and respect for the quality of humble lives which one finds in a poem like "Campos de Soria" [CXIII].

When one remembers the earlier poems, it is as if in *Campos de Castilla* Machado had found a way of confronting the processes of the individual mind with an external reality which, in its turn, could be interpreted in terms of something resembling a collective memory. As Gutiérrez-Girardot says:

> Se trata de la interiorización del paisaje castellano, de la poetización de lo intrahistórico, mediante el cual ese mundo entra ahora a poblar los laberintos y galerías de la memoria y del alma (*11*, 62).

What this transition must have meant for Machado at the time is suggested by a statement he was to make almost twenty years later in *Reflexiones sobre la lírica* (1925):

> Si el soñador despierta, no ya entre fantasmas, sino firmemente anclado en un trozo de lo real, será el respeto cósmico a la ley que nos obliga y nos afirma en nuestro lugar y en nuestro tiempo la fuente de una nueva y severa emoción . . . (*4*, II, 129–30).

In practice, it is often difficult to separate Machado's direct experience of Castile from his awareness of other writers' reactions. The fascination of the Castilian landscape for men like Unamuno and Azorín lay partly in the contrast with their own native regions. (Unamuno was a Basque and Azorín came from the province of Alicante.) Machado, an Andalusian by birth, had left Seville for Madrid at the age of eight. Though later he was to return to the south, the images he carried with him were those of infancy and early childhood:

> Mi infancia son recuerdos de un patio de Sevilla,
> y un huerto claro donde madura el limonero;
> mi juventud, veinte años en tierra de Castilla; . . .
> ("Retrato" [XCVII])*

*It would be interesting to know for certain when this poem was written. Sánchez Barbudo (*13*, 241) says that it is dated 1912 in *Páginas escogidas* (1917), but this is not so. It is hard to imagine Machado writing the

In Madrid, his studies at the Institución Libre de Enseñanza included organized excursions to the country, and especially to the Sierra de Guadarrama. This particular landscape, however, appears only occasionally in his poems, and hardly at all in *Campos de Castilla*. The reason, perhaps, lies in its very familiarity :

> ¿Eres tú, Guadarrama, viejo amigo,
> la sierra gris y blanca,
> la sierra de mis tardes madrileñas
> que yo veía en el azul pintada?
>
> [CIV]

This, in other words, is the landscape Machado had grown up with; as far as one can judge, not even the transition to Soria brought with it the sense of shock one finds in Unamuno or Baroja at being confronted with an unfamiliar region. And conversely, it is only after 1912 that Machado fully encounters the very different atmosphere of Upper Andalusia, though by this stage, as we shall see, the intervening experience of Soria has brought with it new complexities and tensions.

Though Machado is acutely aware of the visual qualities of the Castilian landscape, the main impulse behind his writing is not aesthetic but historical : a sense of history in which the past is judged critically in terms of its relevance to the present. Oddly enough, it is precisely here that Machado begins to move apart from other writers of the 1898 generation. The one he most resembles in his vision of Castile is the Unamuno of *En torno al casticismo* (1895); in Unamuno's later descriptive essays, as in most of Azorín, the note of genuine social criticism is absent or, at the best, overlaid by other, more personal, considerations. As Carlos Blanco Aguinaga has said :

> . . . mientras otros miembros de la generación del 98 evolucionan hacia el subjetivismo, el escepticismo y el esteticismo y,

---

second stanza (". . . . mas recibí la flecha que me asignó Cupido, / y amé cuanto ellas pueden tener de hospitalario") at a time when his wife was mortally ill, and the reference to *modernismo* ("los afeites de la actual cosmética . . .") would have been more pointed a few years earlier. There is a curious resemblance, in both metre and style, to the poem by Manuel Machado, "Adelfos", first published in 1902. Rafael Ferreres (*2a*, 11–12) also argues in favour of an earlier date.

como consecuencia, van a dar a un paisajismo que puede em-
parentarse con la tradición Fernán Caballero – Pereda [i.e.
with nineteenth-century *costumbrismo*, which emphasized the
merely picturesque], Antonio Machado sigue el camino in-
verso, y cuando se ocupa por primera vez del paisaje es ello
para ver con mayor claridad en la España de su tiempo (*8*,
321).

This is why, for Machado, to dwell on the past associations of
such a landscape is ultimately sterile. Only *intrahistoria* persists :
for the rest, a history which is allowed to dominate the present
must be rejected in the interests of the future. At various points,
he seems to suggest that history is a living organism; as he put it
in a speech of 1910 : "Todos sabemos que la historia es algo que
constantemente se altera y modifica."* The poetic version of this
occurs in "El dios ibero" [CI], first published in 1913 :

> ¡Qué importa un día! Está el ayer alerto
> al mañana, mañana al infinito,
> hombres de España, ni el pasado ha muerto,
> ni está el mañana – ni el ayer – escrito.

The distinctive touch comes in the last line : the suggestion that,
beyond any vague hope of a better future, there is a possibility
that the future will make available the true meaning of the past
– a complex interlocking of time which, less openly stated, appears in many of the best poems of *Campos de Castilla*.

To see how these various concerns work together, we can take
one of the most striking poems in the collection, "A orillas del
Duero" [XCVIII], which dates from 1909. The poem opens with
a description :

> Mediaba el mes de julio. Era un hermoso día.
> Yo, solo, por las quiebras del pedregal subía,
> buscando los recodos de sombra, lentamente . . .

The speaker is climbing a hill which looks over the town of
Soria to the country beyond. The tone of this opening is casual,

---

*See Heliodoro Carpintero, "Un texto olvidado: discurso de Antonio
Machado en el homenaje a Pérez de Mata", *La Torre*, XII, 45–6 (1964),
21–38. In the same speech, Machado describes Spain as "un pueblo sin ansias
de renovarse ni respeto a la tradición de sus mayores".

and at first the details hardly seem to compose into a unity. Nevertheless, these apparently casual openings of Machado's often contain more than they seem to; they usually establish a mood from which the rest of the poem follows, and very often there comes a point at which some detail takes on a value beyond its mere function as description. Here, a good deal of the later part of the poem is pessimistic, and part of the purpose of the opening description seems to be to create a mood from which this pessimism can follow. One notices, for example, the emphasis on fatigue: "A trechos me paraba para enjugar mi frente . . .", and so on. When this first appears, it is simply physical; but the way in which the poem develops suggests that this is also a weariness of the spirit, something which is also to some extent identified with the landscape and the various ideas associated with it – above all, the feeling of the decadence of the country. And one notices also how much of the atmosphere of the opening is summed up in "Sobre los agrios campos caía un sol de fuego": the unfertile fields and the merciless sun, isolated in a separate sentence after the sinuous movement of the opening lines.

Machado, then, is creating a mood, and at the same time inviting the reader to share in this mood to the extent of showing him exactly how it came about. By giving us so many details of his experience – not only what he sees, but what he feels (fatigue) and smells (the wild plants), and even the way his body moves – Machado is giving us every opportunity he can of feeling ourselves in his place. This is important, since what the opening description is leading up to is a *viewpoint*. Machado's walk is leading him to an identifiable place – possibly the castle at Soria – from which he can command the landscape, and it is the landscape seen from this particular point which serves as the basis for his reflections. In the opening lines, up to the image of the vulture ("Un buitre de anchas alas con majestuoso vuelo . . ."), we are given a scene in which there is only a single figure – the poet himself. And the appearance of the vulture both sums up the solitariness of the whole passage and adds its own note of ill-omen.

Now the poet has reached his physical vantage-point, the scene widens:

> Yo divisaba, lejos, un monte alto y agudo,
> y una redonda loma cual recamado escudo,
> y cárdenos alcores sobre la parda tierra
> – harapos esparcidos de un viejo arnés de guerra –,
> las serrezuelas calvas por donde tuerce el Duero
> para formar la corva ballesta de un arquero
> en torno a Soria . . .

The most striking effect of this passage is the way it suggests the figure of a warrior. "Suggests" seems the right word, since this is not a very definite image, though a more literal treatment would probably have damaged the tone of the poem. Thus the various components of the landscape taken in turn *seem* to the imagination like the scattered pieces of a warrior's armour. The comparison is deliberately fantastic, but this is surely part of Machado's intention : later in the poem, his imagination is going to take up the theme of the heroic past of Castile, and this acts as a prelude to what is eventually to follow. (Also, of course, the fantastic associations of the scene are given a more concrete basis in the description of Soria itself. The "barbican" image is explained in the prose version of "La tierra de Alvargonzález" : "Soria mística y guerrera, guardaba antaño la puerta de Castilla, como una barbacana hacia los reinos moros que cruzó el Cid en su destierro".) By contrast, the lines which come immediately after this ("Veía el horizonte . . .") refer to the present-day life of the town : the beasts in the fields, the men driving their carts across the bridge into Soria. The details in the last few lines are beautifully concentrated : "carros, jinetes y arrieros", "el largo puente", the shadow which the arches of the bridge cast on the water. And above all, there is the skill with which the whole scene is suddenly brought into focus by the phrase "¡tan diminutos!" – the men like toys in the distance –, an exclamation which, as so often in Machado, carries overtones of surprise and affection.

The rest of the poem, except for the very ending, is quite different. The mood is now established, the physical scene has been evoked, and Machado can let his mind dwell on its meaning. Some of what follows may strike one as over-rhetorical. Here and elsewhere in *Campos de Castilla*, some of the things Machado is saying have dated, or now seem over-simplified, and

the more declamatory parts, though memorable and vigorous in
their own way, are less subtle and well-written than the rest of
the poem. At the same time, it would be wrong to regard such a
passage as a digression: what Machado is saying here is an in-
tegral part of the poem, and to ignore this is to pass over an important dimension of the collection as a whole.* Starting from
the repeated image of the river, the second half of the poem is
built round an obvious contrast between the present decadence of
Spain ("España miserable . . .") and its past greatness. This has
two aspects, religious and military, though in this particular
poem the religious side is only touched on. And perhaps "military" is not quite the right word: Machado is not making an
apology for war, but praising the generosity of the Cid and the
energy of the *conquistadores*.

The present with which this is contrasted is more complex:
first, the general air of dereliction – abandoned fields, ruined
cities, ignorant peasants with no genuine folk culture ("sin dan-
zas ni canciones") –, and the more general complaint against
those who emigrate rather than cultivate their lands. Some of
Machado's fiercest criticisms are directed at what he feels to be
the insularity of Castile. This general indifference to outside ideas
is taken up again near the end, where he refers to the mediocrity
of those who pass for wise men ("Filósofos nutridos de sopa de
convento . . ."); here, the point is that Spain may be compelled
to reckon with the outside world, perhaps in a way she does not
want, under the threat of a European war.†

Nevertheless, Machado's attitude to Spain is not purely nega-
tive. This is clear from the lines which come near the beginning
of the passage:

> ¿Espera, duerme o sueña? ¿La sangre derramada
> recuerda, cuando tuvo la fiebre de la espada?
> Todo se mueve, fluye, discurre, corre o gira;

*Compare Carlos Blanco Aguinaga: "Quien pretenda que estos y otros
poemas pueden eliminarse de una lectura de *Campos de Castilla* atenta
contra lo que se llama unidad e intenta reducir el gran libro al paisajismo
mistificador de los demás . . ." (*8*, 320).

†Machado is referring specifically to the war in Morocco which broke out
in July, 1909.

cambian la mar y el monte y el ojo que los mira.
¿Pasó? Sobre sus campos aún el fantasma yerra
de un pueblo que ponía a Dios sobre la guerra.

The questions, though ambiguous in the context, at least allow the possibility of optimism : Castile may be waiting in hope, not sleeping; she may not have forgotten her aggressiveness in the past. The two lines which follow express, in simple and memorable terms, Machado's sense of historical relativity; all things change : not merely natural objects and elements, but the eye which records them – and, by extension, the mind which shapes them into a pattern of meaning. And so the whole sense of the past is called into question. There is a certain absurdity in the fact that a land of "campos sin arados, regatos ni arboledas" is still haunted by the ghosts of its former splendour, and there is a real fear that the future will continue to be dominated by a past which is no longer related, in any vital sense, to the present. As Concha Zardoya points out : "El paisaje natural se ha convertido en un paisaje histórico : es un ex-paisaje histórico, para ser más exacto" (27, 82). Machado, of course, knows this, and a good deal of the bitterness and melancholy of the poem comes from the recognition. At the same time, concern, for Machado, is seldom far from compassion, the "tristeza que es amor" which he describes in "Campos de Soria" [CXIII].

The poem ends, in fact, on a similar mixture of feelings. The last lines, from "El sol va declinando . . .", are another attempt to create a mood; in a way, a return to the beginning, though now qualified by what has come between. The three central images are clearly distinguished : the "enlutadas viejas" who are imprisoned in the past; the momentary pleasure at seeing the weasels run across the path (perhaps hinting that the natural behaviour of animals is something which is always new, unlike the bitter experience of a society in decline); and, in complete contrast to this, the final picture of the inn open to the dark fields and the deserted rocks. The overall effect is beautifully controlled, and at the same time open-ended – perhaps, Machado might have said, like history itself. The "camino blanco" may be no more than a literal detail, though in Machado roads are often metaphors of the individual life. Most striking of all, though, is the appropriateness with which the poem is brought to rest on the same word — "pedregal" — which had opened the original description : the rocks, associated first of all with the difficult climb to the vantage-point, and now deserted because the speaker has come down again, his moment of vision having passed.

I have dwelt on this poem first, since it shows many of the typical strengths of *Campos de Castilla*, as well as some possible weaknesses. It should be clear by now that Castile, for Machado, is a peopled landscape, and that one of his major problems is to relate the ghosts of a still familiar past to the needs of its present inhabitants. Nevertheless, in his darker moments, it is as if he had recognized that such a problem could hardly have touched the minds of the people most directly concerned. In the speech from which I have already quoted, he registers his sense of dismay at encountering the basic emotions of rural life :

> Y cuando se pasa de las grandes ciudades a las ciudades pequeñas ... y de las ciudades pequeñas a los pueblos ... y de los pueblos a las aldeas y a los campos donde florecen los crímenes sangrientos y brutales, sentimos que crece la hostilidad del medio, se agrava el encono de las pasiones y es más densa y sofocante la atmósfera de odio que se respira.*

In the poems, this sometimes amounts to a sense that the people who live in such surroundings are degraded beyond any hope of redemption; as Aurora de Albornoz puts it : "[El 'hombre de estos campos'] es un hombre incapaz de objetivar el mundo que le rodea; ese páramo terrible es él mismo" (7, 187).

She is referring specifically to the poem "Por tierras de España" [XCIX], originally published in 1910, a few months after "A orillas del Duero". Here, man is inseparable from the landscape — ". . . en páramos malditos trabaja, sufre y yerra" —, and Machado leaves behind all pretence of realism by associating the land itself with the original crime of envy :

> son tierras para el águila, un trozo de planeta
> por donde cruza errante la sombra de Caín.

*See note on p. 23.

One might argue that, in imposing his own myth on what he describes, Machado is falsifying the very reality he is trying to understand. Certainly, in a poem like this, it is hard to draw the line between truth and exaggeration, though some of Unamuno's writings of this period suggest that there was sufficient basis in fact.* From a literary point of view, however, this kind of theme calls for a more dramatic treatment if it is to be entirely convincing – something which Machado was to attempt a few years later in one of his most ambitious poems, "La tierra de Alvargonzález".

On a smaller scale, there are a number of other poems which express, directly or by implication, the weaknesses of the Castilian temperament. "Un criminal" [CVIII], for instance, embodies in a single anecdote the atmosphere of rural vice already sketched out in "Por tierras de España". The waxwork precision with which the various figures are described both distances the event – a murder trial in a provincial town – and surrounds it with a feeling of collective guilt:

> Un pueblo, carne de horca, la severa
> justicia aguarda que castiga al malo.

In a poem like this, Machado is approaching the world of the *romances de ciego* – the popular broadsheet accounts of sensational crimes – which he was to explore still further in "La tierra de Alvargonzález". And, significantly, the crimes in both poems are committed in the same manner and for similar motives: envy, and the desire to inherit at all costs.

A slightly later poem, "El dios ibero" [CI], from which I have already quoted the lines on the fluid quality of history, is for the most part a dramatic monologue placed in the mouth of another generalized figure, the "hombre ibero" of the opening

---

*Compare: "Los crímenes más bestiales, más propios de bestias, de que he podido enterarme desde que vine a esta región—una de las que acusan mayor criminalidad de España—han sido crímenes cometidos en el campo y por campesinos, no en la ciudad, ni por ciudadanos." *Obras completas*, ed. cit., IV, 449–50.

lines.* The device is not altogether successful : as Sánchez Barbudo has pointed out :

> Esta "oración" es ocurrencia irónica de Machado, y no en ver-
> dad la del típico "hombre ibero", pues aunque éste blasfeme
> en ciertas ocasiones y alabe a Dios en otras, no hace probable-
> mente las dos cosas a la vez (*13*, 189).

Nevertheless, though this makes for some confusion, it scarcely
damages the underlying truth of the poem : the perversion of religion for material ends is something Machado had no doubt observed, and the contrast with the more genuine faith of the past
opens naturally into the more hopeful mood of the ending. This
transition is not as obvious as it might appear : Machado is not
saying "religious belief was great in the past and can be great
again"; the "Dios hispano" of the final stanza seems not so
much the God of Christianity as a vision of the ideal Spain of the
future which will be created by the labour of its inhabitants. The
ending, in fact, has less in common with the poems of the Soria
period than with the more socially-committed poems of 1913–15,
such as "El mañana efímero" [CXXXV] and "Una España
joven" [CXLIV]; already the note of summons is becoming
more urgent ("hombres de España, ni el pasado ha muerto . . ."),
just as the denunciation in the earlier part of the poem is less
bound to particular circumstances.†

Machado's revulsion at the more sordid features of rural life is
matched – and, in his finest poems, overcome – by his compassion for certain kinds of individual and by a growing sense
of community. Among the former are the obvious outcasts from
society : the paupers and the mentally deranged. Here, there is
little to qualify the sombre picture of a land dominated by greed
and envy. In "Un loco" [CVI], first published in January, 1913,

---

*The "ballestero / tahur de la cantiga" (lines 1–2) is an allusion to
Cantiga CIV of Alfonso X of Castile (1221–84). Machado uses the same
image in "Desde mi rincón" [CXLIII] : "Contra la flecha que el tahur
tiraba / al cielo, creo en la palabra buena."

†"El dios ibero" was first published in the Soria newspaper *El Porvenir
Castellano* on 5th May, 1913. The lines on chance ("la voltaria rueda / del
año") are echoed in "Poema de un día" [CXXVIII] : "los que hogaño, /
como antaño, / tienen toda su moneda / en la rueda, / traidora rueda del
año".

the setting still seems to be Castile, and Machado reintroduces the hostile image of the centaur which he had already used in "Por tierras de España". What compassion there is lies partly in the honesty of the description and partly in the final reflections on the central figure. The first part of the poem is stark and economical; the interpretation which follows ("Huye de la ciudad . . ."), by contrast, seems forced. In attempting to see the idiot as a victim of urban corruption, Machado is surely superimposing a meaning which scarcely follows from the context, and in doing so, comes dangerously close to cliché. The desire to find an explanation where none is immediately evident leads to a certain senti-mentality ("No fue por una trágica amargura . . .;/purga un pecado ajeno; . . .") which is only partly redeemed by the strength of the last line. What seems most genuine in this pas-sage, on the other hand, is the delicacy of the connection between the idiot's delusion ("a solas con su sombra y su locura") and the visionary light of the day, the "sueño de lirio en lontananza" which hovers over the sterile land.

"El hospicio" [C] is a much more successful poem drawn from a similar area of experience. Here again, one notices Machado's habit of beginning a poem with a simple statement based on the verb "to be": "Es el hospicio, el viejo hospicio provinciano . . ."* On the surface, the first two stanzas seem purely descriptive: in the context of the whole poem, however, the exactness of certain nouns and adjectives ("caserón" . . . "ennegrecidas" . . . "grietados muros y sucios paredones") sug-gests a degree of attention, of alertness to detail, which prepares one for the more subjective mood of the ending. Other touches anticipate this transition: in lines 3–4, the sequence of visual im-pressions is broken by the images of the alternating seasons, which are echoed later by the contrasting kinds of weather ("los montes azules" . . . "los cielos blancos"). More strikingly still, the defining verb "es" is used a second time ("es un rincón de som-bra eterna"), with a significant difference: what it introduces now is not a piece of visual description, but a metaphor which

---

*Compare: "Es una tarde mustia y desabrida . . ." [CVI]; "El acusado es pálido y lampiño . . ." [CVIII]; "Es una hermosa noche de verano . . ." [CXI]; "Es la tierra de Soria árida y fría . . ." [CXIII].

embodies a personal reaction. And this is confirmed, with the same unobtrusive skill, in the exclamation which ends the line. "¡El viejo hospicio!" not merely repeats the earlier phrase, but registers the extent to which the emotional temperature of the poem has been raised as observation has given place to involvement.

The rest of the poem moves forward from this, in what seems a deliberately tentative syntactical pattern:

> Mientras el sol de enero su débil luz envía,
> su triste luz velada sobre los campos yermos, . . .

Here, even more than in the first two stanzas, the beautifully controlled repetitions help to create the slow, reflective tone which runs through the whole poem. The most striking example of this occurs in the last line, the simplicity of which comes as a release after the slightly contorted phrasing which precedes it. A good deal of the strength of these last two stanzas depends on the way in which the first mention of the inhabitants of the poor-house is delayed. The twelfth line – "algunos rostros pálidos, atónitos y enfermos" – is a triumph of compression: the pathos of the several faces pressed into a single window, coupled with the adjective "atónitos", creates an impression of uncomprehending anonymity, as of something perfectly seen but held at a distance. Yet this apparent distancing is deceptive: in what follows, it is the speaker himself who is imagining the world outside – the two distinct kinds of January weather – through the eyes of the occupants, in such a way that *their* "astonishment" becomes his own. Thus the compassion which, in the first half of the poem, was present mainly as an attention to detail emerges, not merely as genuine sympathy for the deprived, but also as a renewed sense of strangeness in the face of a common mortality. It is this sense which is brought out by the repetition in the last line: by choosing to dwell on the second kind of weather, Machado prepares the way for an ending which, as the punctuation suggests, continues to echo beyond the final exclamation mark – a feeling of wonder which, characteristically, goes beyond the powers of actual speech.

In contrast to these last few poems, there are others which

convey a genuine sense of community. This is not so much a question of suppressing the darker tones of a poem like "El hospicio", as of embodying these in a broader vision, in which the rise and fall of human life are played off against the continuing cycle of the seasons. Of the poems included in the original edition of *Campos de Castilla*, the outstanding example of this is "Campos de Soria" [CXIII]. In a slightly earlier piece, "Pascua de resurrección" [CXII], which probably dates from Easter, 1909, one can already sense the kind of connection which Machado was about to explore in the longer poem. Though it seems to hint at a traditional kind of Easter poem, the Christian references are minimal; instead, the invitation to celebrate the season of love and fertility involves not only a sense of continuity but also a dramatic foreshortening of human lives:

> ¿No han de mirar un día, en vuestros brazos,
> atónitos, el sol de primavera,
> ojos que vienen a la luz cerrados,
> y que al partirse de la vida ciegan?*

In "Campos de Soria", the process is more complex, partly because the poem is not bound to a single season and the cyclical movement of the various sections involves a much greater variety of human lives. Of the nine sections, the first four are more of a piece than the rest, though in retrospect their steady plotting of individual moments seems an essential part of the poem as a whole. The first describes the hesitant beginnings of spring – of all times of the year, the one which Machado most often associates with the bare uplands of Soria. The only inhabitants of the landscape are defined in terms of the persisting cold; beside the remaining evidence of winter, the signs of spring are sparse and modest: "la primavera pasa/dejando . . . sus diminutas margaritas blancas". The decisive line comes just after this: "La tierra no revive, el campo sueña". The last phrase here is the first subjective note in the poem and, characteristically, it is ambiguous. Is the countryside "sleeping", as if too numb to change, or is it

---

*Compare: "Que se nos van las Pascuas, mozas, / que se nos va la Pascua a todas" (no. 447 in *Lírica hispánica de tipo popular*, ed. M. Frenk Alatorre, México, 1966), glossed by Góngora in his *romance* "Que se nos va la Pascua, mozas".

"dreaming" of the future? This is not the only poem in which Machado associates "sueño" with the coming of spring. In "Orillas del Duero" [CII], for example, the link is made through a simile:

> ¡Primavera soriana, primavera
> humilde, como el sueño de un bendito,
> de un pobre caminante que durmiera
> de cansancio en un páramo infinito!

The second section of "Campos de Soria" introduces what seems like a variation on this — "Las tierras labrantías . . . siembran/el sueño alegre de infantil Arcadia" —, in which the "dream" is clearly the observer's and the landscape a projection of his own childish illusions. The full implications of this only appear in the final section of the poem: meanwhile, the emphasis has shifted unobtrusively from the overlapping of spring and winter (section I) to the full promise of spring. In a way, it is Machado's gift for organizing the significant details of the scene in sharply-etched phrases ("el huertecillo, el abejar, los trozos/de verde oscuro . . .") which makes possible the innocent vision of Arcadia; at the same time, the simple but telling similes ("como retazos de estameñas pardas" . . . "como un glauco vapor") confirm that this is a landscape which is being explored mentally, in terms of its visual connections.

This desire to encompass the whole landscape in the mind emerges clearly in the third section, where there is a deliberate change of viewpoint half-way through. To begin with, the travellers who ride through the landscape are seen as "plebeyas figurillas" — a phrase which recalls the "¡tan diminutos!" of "A orillas del Duero". The alternating disappearance and reappearance of these figures — at moments silhouetted against the evening sky — presupposes a low angle of vision which is immediately thrown into contrast by the bird's eye view of the closing lines:

> Mas si trepáis a un cerro y veis el campo
> desde los picos donde habita el águila . . .

Here, the summons to the reader ("Mas si trepáis . . . y veis") is an important part of the effect, as if he were being invited to share in the construction of the all-embracing vision; for a moment, the humanized landscape is replaced by an artist's rendering of geology, in which everything is reduced to colour and shifting light.

The fourth section returns to the human scene with a new emotional warmth: "¡Las figuras del campo sobre el cielo!" The season is now autumn: the description of the ploughing scene which follows fills out with a single instance the idea of recurring country tasks and at the same time brings together the beginnings of new life in both man and nature. The closeness of human life to the earth itself is also suggested by the final image: "Bajo una nube de carmín y llama,/... las sombras se agigantan" – the shadows spreading across the field balancing the "figuras ... sobre el cielo" of the opening. Clearly, though the passage is too general to be described as anecdote, the emphasis on a single human group eases the way for the undisguised narrative of the following section. This winter scene contains several echoes of other poems: the snow which falls "como sobre una fosa" recalls the final stanza of "El hospicio", and the crease on the old man's forehead – "tal el golpe de un hacha sobre un leño" – appears again in "La tierra de Alvargonzález" (lines 115–16). Both are images of desolation and loss: the snow which dominates the section from the opening phrase not only cuts off the family from all other human relationships but at some time in the past has broken its unity by depriving it of one of its members. In a sense, the interior fails to act as a refuge from the hostile elements, since these have already marked the lives of the parents: the old man still bears the visible signs of his grief and the listening woman continues to live in the past. Yet the contrast between the generations is quite clear: it is the girl sewing her brightly-coloured dress who looks forward in her imagination to the coming spring, with an obvious echo of the "diminutas margaritas blancas" of the opening section.

The rest of the poem becomes steadily more personal, though, as often happens in Machado, the sense of emotion is conveyed as much by the repeated exclamations as by any direct statements. In the sixth section, the snatch of a traditional rhyme* – "¡Soria

*In fact, the *lema*, or motto, of the town of Soria.

fría, *Soria pura,/cabeza de Extremadura*, . . .!'' – which looks
back to the frontier wars against the Moors, sharply divides the
historical past from the present evidence of decline. In a way, the
opening phrase extends the numbing cold of the winter passage
to the present aspect of the town, as if the chill were a part of
the decadence. The change to a traditional metre adds its own
irony to the description, as does the detail of the "famélicos
galgos" : in actual fact, the stray dogs which run through the
streets, but also suggesting the heraldic hunting-dogs which are
likely to figure on the "escudos/de cien linajes hidalgos". Nevertheless, the impression of the closing lines is one of beauty : despite the neglected appearance of the town, there is, for once, no
note of criticism; whatever its actual qualities, Soria is a "ciudad
castellana", with all the rich overtones of the phrase. And the
additional poignancy comes from the situation of the speaker
himself, from the suggestion of a solitary figure in a particular
place, observing the town by moonlight at a late hour of the
night.

One has only to compare the descriptive passages in the remaining sections with those of the first half to realize how far
the poem has travelled. The seventh section has the effect of
gathering together many of the same impressions ("¡Colinas
plateadas,/grises alcores, cárdenas roquedas . . .") under the stress
of an altogether stronger emotion. Machado's mental map at
this point is still drawn in broad sweeps, as at the end of the
third section; it moves freely between the physical and the historical, with obvious echoes of "A orillas del Duero" (". . . por
donde traza el Duero/su curva de ballesta . . ."), though again
there is no attempt to elaborate the obvious 1898 "topics". Instead, the particulars of the landscape are drawn into a single
complex chord :

> hoy siento por vosotros, en el fondo
> del corazón, tristeza,
> tristeza que es amor!

It is this mood which dominates the rest of the poem and which
gives the closing sections their peculiar strength. So closely, in
fact, does Machado adhere to it that certain words and phrases –

"en el fondo del corazón"; "las rocas sueñan"; "conmigo vais" –
continue to punctuate his final reflections.

In the first half of section VIII, there is a noticeable drop in
tension before the final climax. This seems appropriate enough
in the context: it is as if the increasing intimacy of the poem
had to find its echo in the lives of the people it celebrates, and
Machado's way of achieving this is to seize on the detail of the
lovers' initials cut into the bark of the trees. The season is once
again autumn: by this stage in the poem it scarcely matters
whether the opening sentence – "He vuelto a ver los álamos
dorados . . ." – refers to memory or fact. The sound of the wind
in the leaves blends with that of the river – generally, in these
poems, a symbol of continuity. And it is continuity of a different kind which is stressed in the more emotional passage which
follows, in which the trees – now "álamos del amor" – are seen
as persisting through the seasons. This is one of the gentlest
moments in a poem which, as a whole, seems conceived in a
mood of tenderness and sympathy. What is more important,
however, is the way the impression of the personal lives of the
inhabitants is absorbed into the speaker's own emotion:

> álamos de las márgenes del Duero,
> conmigo vais, mi corazón os lleva!

The simple repetition of "Conmigo vais" leads directly into
the final section. Here, the feeling of expansiveness depends partly
on the movement from the particular to the general – from
"álamos" to "campos de Soria" –, and partly on the sense of a
completed cycle. The latter has more to do with the final reitera-
tion of the central images of the poem – images of both country
and town – than with the actual cycle of the seasons and the
sequence of generations, though these, as we have seen, are an
important part of Machado's feelings. Also, if one reflects on the
final appearance of the word "sueño" – "verde sueño/del suelo
gris y de la parda tierra" –, one realizes how its meaning has
shifted in the course of the poem, from the ambiguous "el campo
sueña" of section I, through the conscious illusion of "el sueño
alegre de infantil Arcadia" (section II), to the "dreaming" rocks
and river of the closing sections. Thus by the end of the poem,

"dream" has become an essential quality of the landscape, just as, one might say, the landscape itself and its people have become an inward part of the poet's own vision. The last four lines of the poem are in the nature of a valedictory wish : a genial address to the people whose landscape this is. The real weight of the ending, however, falls just before this :

> me habéis llegado al alma,
> ¿o acaso estabais en el fondo de ella?

The idea behind these lines takes its richness from the whole poem, and perhaps from the whole of Machado's experience at the time of writing. To put it in its simplest terms, it is as if Machado's feelings about Soria had penetrated his mind so deeply that it is hard to believe that they had not always been there – perhaps in the sense of his own reference to "el sueño alegre de infantil Arcadia". Again, in a fairly literal way, we might read into these lines an awareness of poetic fulfilment : the idea that the experience of Soria made possible a kind of poetry which Machado had already begun to conceive at an earlier stage. Yet, most profoundly of all, there is an implication that Machado himself may not have been fully aware of at the time, though it was greatly to concern him in later years : the sense in which his own temperament ensured that any consistent attempt at "objectivity" was bound to break down in the end under the pressure of his own subjective cast of mind. In "Campos de Soria", the fact that it appears to do so is a strength rather than a fault : the tension, at all events, is beautifully maintained and the final questioning both moving and dramatically exact.

Of all the poems in the 1912 edition, "Campos de Soria" is the one in which Machado seems most acutely aware of the complexity of the relationship between the poet and external reality. As Helen Grant has pointed out, there is much more to the poem than a simple projection of the poet's state of mind on to a particular landscape :

> por su manera de acercarse a la realidad de las cosas, de la gente, o del paisaje, Machado parece buscar en ellas no sólo el reflejo de su propio sentimiento, o un sentimiento genérico, sino el ser auténtico y único de las cosas y su lugar en el esquema del cosmos (22, 469).

In some of the less ambitious poems – for example, "En Abril las aguas mil" [CV] and "Amanecer de otoño" [CIX] – the "objectivity" of the writing seems almost complete. In the first of these, only the suggestion of the poet's presence behind the window – "La lluvia da en la ventana/y el cristal repiquetea" – interrupts the accurate registering of the visible scene; in the second, what emotion there is comes simply from the sense of being present in a certain place at a particular moment. This connects with something we have already seen in Machado's earlier poetry, with the idea of the poet as a solitary traveller or observer. And this in turn is related to one of the most distinctive qualities of Machado's solitude : his sense of wonder. Or, as Gutiérrez-Girardot puts it :

> En él, la soledad es un estado de incesante pasmo y de extrañeza ante el hecho de que el mundo es como es, de que simplemente es mundo. El poeta Machado no está solo o abandonado, más bien es un extranjero en la tierra . . ., un sorprendido espectador (11, 33–9).

This helps to explain the sense of mystery, of something which constantly escapes definition, which suffuses even the most apparently literal descriptions. In one of the poems from *Soledades*, *galerías y otros poemas* to which I have already referred – "¿Mi corazón se ha dormido?" [LX] –, Machado's choice of terms seems especially striking:

> [Mi corazón] Ni duerme ni sueña, mira,
>   los claros ojos abiertos,
>   señas lejanas y escucha
>   a orillas del gran silencio.

The "seeing heart", in other words, fixes its attention on "distant signs" and at the same time "listens" at the borders of silence. What the heart "sees", therefore, is a special aspect of external reality: not simply the appearance of things, but things whose significance is somehow connected with their remoteness.

Because of this, it is perhaps not surprising that so many of Machado's poetic descriptions should have the effect of something deliberately held at a distance, as if the gap between the poet and what he is seeing were responsible for a certain strangeness in what, on the surface, seems a straightforward experience. One of the poems which shows this most clearly is "Noche de verano" [CXI]. Here, the initial distancing is accomplished by a device we have already seen at work in other poems: the defining effect of the verb "to be" ("Es una hermosa noche de verano . . ."), followed by a series of simple statements ("Tienen las altas casas . . ."; "dibujan/sus negras sombras"), in which the verbs pass almost unnoticed among the succession of nouns. Definition, that is to say, consists for the most part of the naming of certain states or objects. If we call such writing "descriptive", it is mainly in the sense that the poet appears to be transcribing a natural and self-sufficient arrangement in which his own presence is scarcely felt. It is only, in fact, in the last two lines that this presence becomes explicit:

> Yo en este viejo pueblo paseando
> solo, como un fantasma.

Yet the very terms of the self-description – "paseando solo"; "como un fantasma" – increase the sense of distance. In the context of the whole poem, it is clear that the image of the town, which already possesses a certain remoteness, is made to recede

further by being associated with the still more distant figure of
the poet. As in other poems of the same kind, what passes across
the gap created by distance is a sense of wonder at being there at
all – emphasized in this particular instance by the image of the
poet-as-revenant.

This is not the only poem of *Campos de Castilla* in which an
apparently "objective" description ends by assuming an almost
dream-like quality. As Zubiría has observed :

> la visión que tenía Machado del mundo exterior, de su circun-
> stancia, era una visión de marcado acento onírico [i.e. dream-
> like]; de mundo soñado, y que, a veces, sueña; de mundo como
> sueño . . . En lo que concierne a la realidad interior, los tér-
> minos de la proposición se invierten, y entonces nos encon-
> tramos con que el sueño también es un mundo, que nada le
> faltaba para serlo : topografía, paisajes, habitantes, etc. (*15*,
> 92–3).

The lines I have already quoted from "Campos de Soria" – "me
habéis llegado al alma,/¿o acaso estabais en el fondo de ella?" –
seem to confirm this; at the same time, a good deal of *Campos de
Castilla* is an attempt to do justice to the intrinsic qualities of
what lies outside the poet, without recourse to introspection.

As we have seen, Machado's awareness of the problems involved in the relationship between the poet and his environment
goes back a long way. His best-known attempt at a theoretical
formulation occurs in the preface he wrote to *Páginas escogidas*
(1917) :

> Somos víctimas – pensaba yo – de un doble espejismo. Si mira-
> mos afuera y procuramos penetrar en las cosas, nuestro mundo
> externo pierde en solidez, y acaba por disipársenos cuando
> llegamos a creer que no existe por sí, sino por nosotros. Pero si,
> convencidos de la íntima realidad, miramos adentro, entonces
> todo nos parece venir de fuera, y es nuestro mundo interior
> nosotros mismos, lo que se desvanece. ¿Qué hacer, entonces?
> Tejer el hilo que nos dan, soñar nuestro sueño, vivir; sólo así
> podremos obrar el milagro de la generación. Un hombre atento
> a sí mismo y procurando auscultarse ahoga la única voz que
> podría escuchar : la suya; pero le aturden los ruidos extraños.
> ¿Seremos, pues, meros espectadores del mundo? Pero nuestros
> ojos están cargados de razón y la razón analiza y disuelve.

Pronto veremos el teatro en ruinas, y, al cabo, nuestra sola sombra proyectada en la escena. Y pensé que la misión del poeta era inventar nuevos poemas de lo eterno humano, historias animadas que, siendo suyas, viviesen, no obstante, por sí mismas.

It is likely that Machado would not have expressed the problem in quite such metaphysical terms at the time of writing the poems he included in the first edition of *Campos de Castilla*. Nevertheless, the basic terms of the paradox are sufficiently close to the actual sense of the poems. The danger, he is saying, is that, by reflecting on the world outside himself, the poet will defeat the whole object of his enquiry: to see things as they really are, without the mediation of his own thoughts. Conversely, excessive introspection – and here one remembers his earlier reaction to the *Galerías* poems – may drown the poet's sense of his own voice by destroying the only firm centre from which it can come. Expressed in these terms, the dilemma is virtually insoluble: what Machado seems to fear most of all is that over-consciousness – whether directed inwardly or outwardly – will inhibit the true sources of poetic creation. The remedy he suggests – "Tejer el hilo que nos dan, soñar nuestro sueño, vivir" – is understandably vague: to make the best of what one is given, to trust in one's own vision without analysing it too much, and simply to "live". The important thing, for Machado, is the kind of poem which it remains possible to write, the "nuevos poemas de lo eterno humano" of the final sentence.

The passage which follows refers directly to the most ambitious poem of the collection:

Me pareció el romance la suprema expresión de la poesía y quise escribir un nuevo Romancero. A este propósito responde "La tierra de Alvargonzález".

Machado's preference for the ballad is logical enough if one bears in mind his previous argument. If his ideal at this stage was to create poems which would appear to exist independently of their author, the advantages of an invented narrative based on a timeless human situation must have seemed immensely attractive. There is no doubt, either, that such a project must have seemed close to another of Machado's ideals: the possibility of writing a more public kind of poetry which would embody the collective concerns of a whole people. In order to achieve this, he rejects any idea of writing pastiche:

> . . . mis romances no emanan de las heroicas gestas, sino del pueblo que las compuso y de la tierra donde se cantaron; mis romances miran a lo elemental humano, al campo de Castilla y al Libro Primero de Moisés, llamado Génesis.

The implications of this should become clear when we consider the poem itself. As a preliminary, however, it is worth recounting the facts of its composition, since these tell us a good deal about Machado's intentions. "La tierra de Alvargonzález" exists in three versions, one in prose and two in verse. The prose version was originally published in the January, 1912, number of *Mundial Magazine*, a Spanish-language periodical edited in Paris by Rubén Darío. The poem itself appeared for the first time in the Madrid literary journal *La Lectura* in April of the same year, to be followed a few weeks later by the definitive version included in the first edition of *Campos de Castilla*. The differences between the two poetic versions, though significant, are less striking than those between the poem and the original prose sketch. In the latter, the whole story is set in an objective framework by the introduction of a second narrator: the author's own account of a journey to the source of the River Duero is made to include the legend of Alvargonzález, which is told to him by a peasant he meets on the way, who in his turn has heard it in his childhood from a shepherd. (Though it seems certain that the story was invented by Machado, he is known to have made a similar journey himself in the autumn of 1910.) This choice of an uneducated narrator imposes certain conditions on the story: compared with the poetic versions, there is much less description, and a greater tendency to comment explicitly on the workings of fear and guilt.* Moreover, the story itself differs in one important detail: the fact that the murderers also kill their younger brother, Miguel.

*For example: "Difícil es interpretar los sueños que desatan el haz de nuestros propósitos para mezclarlos con recuerdos y temores" and "La maldad de los hombres es como la Laguna Negra, que no tiene fondo".

Each of these differences in its way reflects a change of emphasis in the poetic versions.* To take the last point, the suppression of the second murder not only simplifies the plot, but concentrates the interest on the pattern of retribution which derives from the single crime. This greater or lesser economy depends partly on the relative possibilities of the two media: generally speaking, the prose account tends to explain far more than the poem; the peasant narrator is less directly involved in the events he is retelling than the speaker of the poem, and less concerned with building up an atmosphere of tension. The success of the prose account is largely a question of the way Machado creates a "voice" which combines matter-of-fact realism with traditional country wisdom in the face of the irrational. Thus, in the prose version, Alvargonzález's dream of Jacob's ladder is given a realistic interpretation:

> Y Alvargonzález soñó que una voz le hablaba, y veía como Jacob una escala de luz que iba del cielo a la tierra. Sería tal vez la franja del sol que filtraban las ramas del olmo,

and the brothers' vision of the dead father working in the fields by moonlight ("Los asesinos", II) is explained by their drunkenness. Given the mentality of the narrator, such touches are completely convincing in their context. What one misses in the prose version, on the other hand, is the whole dimension of Castile – largely, though not entirely, a matter of description –, and the haunting ambiguity of much of the poem. As Allen Phillips has said: "El verso acentúa lo sobrenatural, la prosa lo natural" (25, 132), and this is a distinction which affects not only the general impression, but many of the individual details.

In the prose version, Machado deliberately associates the story of Alvargonzález with the tradition of the *romances de ciego*:

---

*The main differences between the poem as printed in *Campos de Castilla* and the *La Lectura* version are as follows: (i) the addition of the dedication to Juan Ramón Jiménez and of the section titles; (ii) the addition of sections II-V of "Otros días" and the lines "tierras pobres, tierras tristes, / tan tristes que tienen alma" [566–7] and "¡Oh pobres campos malditos, / pobres campos de mi patria!" [575–6]; (iii) the frequent division of the original stanzas into shorter units. For other verbal changes, see the notes to Macrí's edition (2).

> Siendo niño [his narrator says], oí contar a un pastor la his-
> toria de Alvargonzález, y sé que anda inscrita en papeles y que
> los ciegos la cantan por tierras de Berlanga.*

In their typical form, such poems are of no literary value; on the
other hand, as Machado fully realized, they express a genuinely
popular reaction to crime and violence, that is to say, to the
themes which, in the popular imagination, have replaced the
more "heroic" subject-matter of the traditional ballads. This, at
least, is what he seems to imply in the preface of 1917. His problem, one could argue, was to write a poem which would reflect
the popular imagination while avoiding both the anachronisms
of the traditional ballad and the crudities of the *romances de ciego*
themselves. Roughly speaking, his way of doing this is to take an
incident of a type common in the *romances de ciego* and to present it with the full resources of his literary skill, emphasizing
precisely those timeless qualities – "lo eterno humano" – which
he refers to in his preface.

This accounts for the richness of associations which is apparent
from the opening lines:

> Siendo mozo Alvargonzález,
> dueño de mediana hacienda,
> que en otras tierras se dice
> bienestar y aquí opulencia,
> en la feria de Berlanga
> prendóse de una doncella,
> y la tomó por mujer
> al año de conocerla.
> Muy ricas las bodas fueron,
> y quien las vio las recuerda;
> sonadas las tornabodas
> que hizo Alvar en su aldea;
> hubo gaitas, tamboriles,
> flauta, bandurria y vihuela,
> fuegos a la valenciana
> y danza a la aragonesa.

[1-16]

*In the third paragraph of the prose version, there is a reference to a
murder which took place "en los pinares de Durcielo". As Helen Grant
points out (23, 145), this is a veiled allusion to a real crime which was
committed at Duruelo, near Soria, in July, 1910.

The whole passage is full of literary echoes: "Alvargonzález" suggests similar names in the twelfth-century *Cantar de Mio Cid* (Alvar Díaz, Alvar Fáñez), which also refers to Berlanga; the description of the wedding feast has parallels both in the traditional ballads and in certain plays of Lope de Vega, notably *Peribáñez y el Comendador de Ocaña*, while the list of musical instruments recalls a famous passage in the *Libro de Buen Amor* (c. 1330) of Juan Ruiz, Arcipreste de Hita.* Clearly, the effect of such allusions is to create a sense of traditional ritual which surrounds Alvargonzález himself in an atmosphere of patriarchal authority. In the rest of the poem, such literary echoes are comparatively rare: what replaces them is a series of references to Biblical themes and situations. This, of course, is in keeping with Machado's remarks in his preface:

> . . . mis romances miran a lo elemental humano, al campo de
> Castilla y al Libro Primero de Moisés, llamado Génesis.†

To begin with, the curse of Cain, which Machado refers to in other poems of *Campos de Castilla*, now dominates both the general situation ("Mucha sangre de Caín/tiene la gente labriega . . ." [25–6]) and the fortunes of a particular family ("A los Alvargonzález/maldijo Dios en sus tierras . . ." [297–8]). Alongside these, there are other echoes of the Old Testament, all of which tend to reinforce the patriarchal status of Alvargonzález: Jacob's dream, the theme of the favourite child, and the suggestion of the prodigal son in the return of the youngest brother.‡

The ultimate effect of this technique is to increase the horror of the parricide: by introducing this kind of resonance, Machado is raising a sordid local crime to the status of a universal myth,

---

*See *Libro de Buen Amor*, stanzas 1228–34. The name "Peribáñez" actually appears in the prose version. The *copla* which occurs later in the poem—"A la orilla de la fuente / lo asesinaron. / ¡Qué mala muerte le dieron / los hijos malos!" [428–32]—recalls the famous lines from Lope de Vega's play *El caballero de Olmedo:* "Que de noche le mataron / al caballero, / la gala de Medina, / la flor de Olmedo."

†It seems clear that Machado regarded the poem as a series of ballads— a *romancero*—, rather than as a single ballad.

‡There is possibly also an allusion to Pharaoh's dream (*Genesis*, ch. xli) in the lines "Así, a un año de pobreza / siguió un año de pobreza" [287–8].

in which the offence against the nature of the family sets up a
timeless pattern of guilt and retribution. At the same time, a
great deal of this process depends on the actual way in which the
story is told. In the early stages of the poem – up to the fifth
section of "Aquella tarde" – we seem to be in the presence of an
omniscient narrator, of a speaker who is in full command of the
events he is describing. The "voice" which Machado has created
for the poem – unlike that of the peasant narrator in the prose
version – moves easily between literary allusion and the type of
comment one associates with the oral tradition ("Muy ricas las
bodas fueron/*y quien las vio las recuerda*"). Compared with the
prose version, there is a fine economy, particularly in the account
of the dream, and the suppression of circumstantial detail from
time to time creates an effect of ominous understatement.* One
can also point to the skill with which Machado has transposed
some of his original material: for example, an over-explicit sentence in the prose version – "El agua que brotaba en la piedra
parecía relatar una historia vieja y triste: la historia del crimen
en el campo" – becomes "Cuenta la hazaña del campo/el agua
clara corriendo", and this is placed *after* the description of the
murder. (These last verses are the first indication of a theme
which is to dominate the later stages of the poem: the idea that
nature and human lives run in parallel, and that the elements of
the landscape are an active reminder of the brothers' guilt.) It is
the fifth section, however, which is decisive:

> Pasados algunos meses,
> la madre murió de pena.
> Los que muerta la encontraron
> dicen que las manos yertas
> sobre su rostro tenía,
> oculto el rostro con ellas.

[151–6]

---

*Compare the ending of the dream in the prose version—"Soñaba
Alvargonzález que sus hijos venían a matarle, y al abrir los ojos vio que era
cierto lo que soñaba"—with the same moment in the poem: "Soñando está
con sus hijos, / que sus hijos lo apuñalan; / y cuando despierta mira /
que es cierto lo que soñaba" [117–20].

The important word is "dicen" : by admitting the possibility of
hearsay, the narrator has abandoned his omniscient rôle and
from now on he will be telling the story, not as it necessarily
happened, but as it exists in the popular mind. The story, in
other words, will no longer pretend to be an eye-witness account,
but will take the form of a legend, in which nature will add its
own voice to that of popular superstition.

One of the the things which make for the power of the narrative is the way in which it shows the legend actually taking shape.
This is particularly obvious in the next part of the poem ("Otros
días"), the last four sections of which were added to the version
published in *La Lectura*. The one section originally included
ends with the lines :

> La tierra de Alvargonzález
> se colmará de riqueza;
> muerto está quien la ha labrado,
> mas no le cubre la tierra.

This, in the earlier context, reads like a bitter reflection on the
part of the speaker : in the expanded version, however, it becomes an independent *copla*, repeated in turn by disembodied
voices, and finally by the river itself. Machado, in other words,
is exploiting the possibilities implied in the passage which comes
immediately after the murder – "Cuenta la hazaña del campo/el
agua clara corriendo . . ." – by inventing a genuinely popular
refrain which is made to hover ambiguously between the landscape itself and the haunted consciences of the brothers. As
Sánchez Barbudo observes :

> En el poema, pues, el poeta expresa sus sentimientos, y éstos
> parecen reflejarse *luego* en lo que el pueblo dice. Pero el pro-
> ceso ocurre en verdad más bien a la inversa : el poeta expresa
> lo que el pueblo previamente ha sentido, o pudo haber sen-
> tido (*13*, 221).

From now on, the poem moves through an alternating sequence of descriptions and anecdotes. The hostile nature which
appears in the account of the brothers' journey at nightfall
("Otros días", III–IV) returns in a different form in the next
section ("Castigo"), which describes the "curse" which has fallen

on their lands. Remorse seems inevitably linked to the winter :
and it is precisely at this dead point in the story that their
younger brother returns. Once again, there is an effect similar to
that of the repeated *copla*. It is the speaker himself who first refers
to the "curse" : "A los dos Alvargonzález/maldijo Dios en sus
tierras" [297–8] ; later, when Miguel's success as a farmer has
emphasized his brothers' failure, it is popular superstition which
draws the same conclusion :

> y ya de aldea en aldea
> se cuenta como un milagro
> que los asesinos tienen
> la maldición en sus campos.

[423–6]

And immediately after this comes the longer and more explicit
version of the *copla* ("A la orilla de la fuente . . . el que la tierra
ha labrado" [429–36]), which in its turn is overheard by Miguel
[444–8].

With this, another stage in the poem is completed. The facts
of the crime, betrayed in the first place by the voice of the water,
are now common knowledge; in a sense, what we have seen is
the creation of a popular *copla* which, once it begins to circulate,
appears to take on a life of its own. Another variant of this *copla*
occurs at the end of the long passage describing the family house
("La casa", I, 517–22). The words which introduce it – "Hoy
canta el pueblo una copla/que va de aldea en aldea . . ." – are ambiguous : the effect of "hoy" may simply be to return us to the
present stage in the narrative after the memories of Alvargonzález's youth; alternatively, it may refer to the speaker's own
present, in other words, to a song which still persists after the
final outcome of the tale. If this were so, it would make a logical
climax to the growing power of the *copla*; whatever the truth,
the following section ("La casa", II) moves into the present in a
different way, as the descriptive writing detaches itself more and
more from the narrative. This effect seems quite deliberate on
Machado's part, since the lines "¡tierras pobres, tierras tristes,/
tan tristes que tienen alma!" [565–6] and "¡oh pobres campos
malditos,/pobres campos de mi patria!" [576–7] appear only in

the definitive version of the poem. For an instant, it is as though the reflective poet of "Campos de Soria" had taken over from the speaker of the ballad – a memorable moment in itself, though one which threatens to destroy the whole fabric of the fiction.

The next part, "La tierra", returns to the narrative and to the effects of the "curse". The final variant of the *copla* – "Cuando el asesino labre/será su labor pesada . . ."[599–602] – strikes a note of ancient prophecy which is fulfilled in the supernatural events of the poem. These – the furrow which closes as soon as it is opened, the soil which flows with blood like a wound – create an effect of mounting horror as the brothers are finally trapped in their guilt. The claustrophobic atmosphere of the closing sections owes a good deal to the verbal echoes of the original crime: "la luna llena, manchada/de un arrebol purpurino" [107–8; 609–10] and "A la vera de la fuente . . ." [121; 647]. These reminders of their guilt are reinforced by the vision of their dead father working in the fields by moonlight. By this stage in the poem, it hardly matters whether such things are "real" or merely projections of their own consciences; the obvious superiority of the poem over the prose version at this point lies in its power to make the irrational convincing. The motive for the brothers' final journey is never explained and it is hard to know to what extent, if any, their death is premeditated. What remains in the mind, however, is the hostile landscape, distorted still further by their tortured imagination, and the finality with which they are engulfed by the impassive lake.

Any description of "La tierra de Alvargonzález" runs the risk of oversimplifying, if only because of the sheer length of the original. The pattern I have tried to bring out is an important one, though it does not account for everything in the poem and possibly makes the construction appear tighter than it actually is. Ultimately, however, one's difficulties in coming to terms with the poem come, not from its length, but from the problem of deciding where its central interest lies. Are we to read it mainly as a story of crime and retribution, or as an attempt to reconstruct the growth of a legend in the popular mind? Or can one claim, as Helen Grant does, that the core of the poem consists of its "evocation of Castile" (*23*, 155)? There is a good deal to be

said for this last view. It is clear that much of the best writing in
the poem occurs in the long descriptive passages, notably in "La
casa" and the opening sections of "Otros días". Here, one is
struck, not only by the resemblances to other poems of *Campos
de Castilla*, but by the way in which the vocabulary itself seems
to increase in density under the pressure of the verse form:

> En laderas y en alcores,
> en ribazos y cañadas,
> el verde nuevo y la hierba,
> aún del estío quemada,
> alternan; los serrijones
> pelados, las lomas calvas,
> se coronan de plomizas
> nubes apelotonadas;
> y bajo el pinar gigante,
> entre las marchitas zarzas
> y amarillentos helechos,
> corren las crecidas aguas
> a engrosar el padre río
> por canchales y barrancas.

[545–58]

Again, and particularly in the definitive version, Machado seems
concerned to extend the implications of the particular situation
and to equate the "pobres campos malditos" of Alvargonzález
with the whole of Castile. This subjective intervention, as we
have seen, is somewhat at odds with the rest of the poem, and it
seems to indicate a basic uncertainty in Machado's intentions.
And this, I think, is the trouble with the poem as a whole: in
spite of many fine passages, these never quite cohere into a single
convincing pattern. The "evocation of Castile" is superbly accomplished, but in a way which cannot help but interfere with
the narrative itself. The narrative thrust, which is so splendidly
sustained in the opening sections, decreases after the death of the
mother and, though it reappears from time to time in the rest
of the poem, seems unable to regain its original intensity.

The intention which Machado expressed in his preface of 1917
– "inventar nuevos poemas de lo eterno humano, historias animadas que, siendo suyas [i.e. the poet's], viviesen, no obstante,

por sí mismas" – presupposes something rather different. As Gutiérrez-Girardot remarks:

> . . . el poema con el que quiso satisfacer este postulado, "La tierra de Alvargonzález", no cumplió las condiciones enunciadas por Machado. La historia del poema no vive por sí misma, sino de la tensión que quería superar (*11*, 23).

This tension is the one he describes earlier in the same preface, and which can be found in other poems of *Campos de Castilla*: the difficulty of perceiving the true nature of reality without the mediation of the reflecting mind. "La tierra de Alvargonzález" shows this problem in a particularly acute form. Though he never repeated the experiment, there can be no doubt that, in turning to the ballad, Machado's instincts were leading him in the right direction: the ballad, because of its dramatic nature, entails a kind of objectivity which is hardly possible in the lyric. Where the poem fails, on the other hand, is precisely in its refusal to limit itself to what is inherently dramatic, however impressive the non-dramatic elements may be in themselves.

4 Leonor

Machado's best comment on his years in Soria occurs in a little-known interview of 1938:

> Soy hombre extraordinariamente sensible al lugar en que vivo.
> La geografía, las tradiciones, las costumbres de las poblaciones
> por donde paso, me impresionan profundamente y dejan huella
> en mi espíritu. Allá, en 1907, fuí destinado como catedrático a
> Soria. Soria es lugar rico en tradiciones poéticas. Allí nace el
> Duero, que tanto papel juega en nuestra historia. Allí, entre
> San Esteban de Gormaz y Medinaceli, se produjo el monu-
> mento literario del Poema del Cid. Por si ello fuera poco,
> guardo de allí el recuerdo de mi breve matrimonio con una
> mujer a la que adoré con pasión y que la muerte me arrebató
> al poco tiempo. Y "viví y sentí" aquel ambiente con toda in-
> tensidad. Subí al Urbión, al nacimiento del Duero. Hice excur-
> siones a Salas, escenario de la trágica leyenda de los Infantes
> [de Lara]. Y de allí nació el poema de Álvargonzález (quoted
> *14*, 54).

Much of this confirms what we have already seen in the poems:
the unusual sensitivity to place, and the awareness that Soria
and its surroundings are charged with associations from the past,
both historical and literary. It is much more difficult, on the
other hand, to gauge the extent to which Machado's personal life
affected the poems of these years. The facts are simple and tragic.
In July, 1909, Machado, who was then thirty-four, married a girl
of sixteen, Leonor Izquierdo Cuevas, whom he had met shortly
after arriving in Soria. Early in 1911, they travelled to Paris,
where Machado attended the lectures of the philosopher Henri
Bergson at the Sorbonne and probably completed one of the versions of "La tierra de Alvargonzález". In July of the same year,
while still in Paris, Leonor was stricken with tuberculosis, and
died a year later (1st August, 1912), just a few weeks after the
publication of *Campos de Castilla*. As we shall see, some of
Machado's most moving poems were written in the months

following his wife's death. By contrast, however, their relationship – though by all accounts an extremely happy one – scarcely enters into the poems written before 1912. This is not so surprising if one bears in mind Machado's mistrust of introspection or, what is perhaps more relevant, his need to come to terms gradually with new experience.* There is, however, one partial exception to this : the poem "A un olmo seco" [CXV], written in May, 1912 – too late to be included in the first edition of *Campos de Castilla*.

One says "partial exception", since it would be perfectly possible to read this poem simply as a lament for the passage of time, based on the symbol of the withered elm-tree. This in itself is a central concern in Machado's poetry as a whole, and in his later prose writings he remarks again and again on the need to stress the element of time in one's poems. In one of the aphorisms of *Nuevas canciones* (1924), Machado defines poetry as "palabra en el tiempo" ("De mi cartera", I), and in *Juan de Mairena* (1928), the same conception emerges in one of his most famous paradoxes :

La poesía es – decía Mairena – el diálogo del hombre, de un hombre con su tiempo. Eso es lo que el poeta pretende eternizar, sacándolo fuera del tiempo, labor difícil y que requiere mucho tiempo, casi todo el tiempo de que el poeta dispone (*4*, II, 180).

Linked with this is the idea that a good poem should represent the fluid nature of experience, the fact that the future is always turning into the present and the present into the past, but that these three stages of time are always interacting in one's mind. Yet, as Machado sees, there is a limit to the amount of actual experience which a poem can convey. The degree of selection which any poem involves means creating a particular pattern – the structure of the poem –, so that the most the poet can do is to emphasize the time-factor within these limits.

"A un olmo seco" shows Machado doing this with marvellous

---

*At one point in his notebooks, he remarks : "Toda composición requiere, por lo menos, diez años para producirse" (*3*, 16).

skill. To begin with, the time-element is part of the subject itself. It is not just that the tree has grown old, but that it is seen clearly in relation to past, present and future. The present is the moment at which the poet is observing it, though the last few lines, as we shall see, suggest a different kind of a relationship, in which the tree comes to symbolize the personal situation of the writer. The opening lines give us its past, and, appropriately, the weight of the description falls on past participles: ". . . *hendido* por el rayo/y en su mitad *podrido*,/. . . algunas hojas verdes le han *salido*." Its future is presented as a series of alternative possibilities – speculations in the mind of the observer –, bound together by a strong syntactical pattern: the repetition of "Antes que . . .", followed by "quiero recordar . . .". In other words, the tree is seen, not as a static object, but as something which is changing under the action of time.

This general impression is carried into many of the details of the poem, particularly into the pattern of shifting tenses which knits together the different moments of time: "le han salido . . . le mancha la corteza . . . No será . . . Antes que te derribe . . .". Also, though this is not something which Machado insists on in his theorizing, there are points in the poem at which space is almost as important as time. In his best poems, from *Soledades* onwards, Machado often plunges us abruptly into a particular setting, a "space" which itself is often charged with emotion or which in some way channels the speaker's own emotions and transmits them as part of a strong visual impression.* So here, the opening lines of the poem focus straight on to "algunas hojas verdes", and further on, there is an alternating series of broad gestures and closely observed details which pull the attention back to the actual object. Each time this happens, we are made more strongly aware of both place and time:

> ¡El olmo centenario en la colina
> que lame el Duero! Un musgo amarillento
> le mancha la corteza blanquecina
> al tronco carcomido y polvoriento.

*On this point, see Dámaso Alonso, *16*, 168–75.

And again:

> No será, cual los álamos cantores
> que guardan el camino y la ribera,
> habitado de pardos ruiseñores.
>
> Ejército de hormigas en hilera
> va trepando por él, y en sus entrañas
> urden sus telas grises las arañas.

Without going any further, we can probably agree that this particular poem observes the conditions which Machado implies when he writes, for example, that "El poema que no tenga muy marcado el acento temporal estará más cerca de la lógica que de la lírica" (4, II, 137). At the same time, of course, it is not a purely descriptive poem: near the end, the relation between the poet and the object he is describing is put very forcefully: "quiero anotar en mi cartera"; and this direct intervention of the poet affects the whole question of what the poem is about. The personal reflection in the closing lines colours in retrospect the whole of the previous description. And this forces us to revise our idea of the poem's "subject", and to think of it, not as the actual physical subject – the dying tree – but as the sum of everything which the assimilation of this concrete fact has enabled the poet to say about his hopes and his sadness. Both kinds of emotion seem sufficiently accounted for in the earlier part of the poem: the surprise at finding new life springing from what, to all appearances, is dead, and the desire to perpetuate this glimpse of transient beauty. Without the last three lines, however, the feelings embodied in the rest of the poem may seem excessive, just as the final expression of hope may strike one as vague without further knowledge of the circumstances. This knowledge is provided, or at least hinted at, by the date of the poem.[*] Machado, in other words, is writing at the time when his wife was mortally ill. As Sánchez Barbudo has noticed, the parallel between the "rama verdecida" and the hope of Leonor's recovery cannot be exact, since the branch is sure to die:

---

[*]When first published in *El Porvenir Castellano* (20-ii-1913), it was dated "Soria, 4 de mayo de 1912".

El "otro milagro" que ahora espera no es, ni mucho menos,
exactamente como el primero : habría de ser un milagro mucho
mayor, mucho más completo . . . Al pensar en Leonor, es puro
verdecer, sin cerco ya de la muerte, lo que su corazón espera
(*13*, 246).

Machado's reticence here is paralleled in several of the poems
written after his wife's death. Wherever it appears, the effect is
of a grief which is afraid to make itself felt in more direct terms
— not so much the "stoicism" of which critics tend to speak, as
a suffering which knows itself to be ultimately incapable of com-
munication.

Machado left Soria eight days after the death of Leonor, and
by November, 1912, had moved to Baeza, in the northern part
of Andalusia, where he was to remain, with few breaks, until
1919. Sometime in 1913 he attempted to describe the effect of his
wife's death in a letter to Unamuno :

La muerte de mi mujer dejó mi espíritu desgarrado. Mi mujer
era una criatura angelical segada por la muerte cruelmente. Yo
tenía adoración por ella : pero sobre el amor está la piedad. Yo
hubiera preferido mil veces morirme a verla morir, hubiera
dado mil vidas por la suya. No creo que haya nada extraor-
dinario en este sentimiento mío. Algo inmortal hay en nosotros
que quisiera morir con lo que muere. Tal vez por esto viniera
Dios al mundo. Pensando en esto, me consuelo algo. Tengo a
veces esperanza. Una fe negativa es también absurda. Sin em-
bargo el golpe fue terrible y no creo haberme repuesto. Mien-
tras luché a su lado contra lo irremediable, me sostenía la conciencia de sufrir mucho más que ella, pues ella, al fin, no
pensó nunca en morirse y su enfermedad no era dolorosa. En
fin, hoy vive en mí más que nunca y algunas veces creo fir-
memente que la he de recobrar. Paciencia y humildad (*3*, 168).

The mood of this letter is reflected in the group of short poems
[CXIX–CXXIV] written about the same time. Several of these
alternate between a feeling of loss and the sense that in some way
Leonor is still present. Though her memory is inseparable from
the landscape of Soria, there is one poem in particular – "Soñé
que tú llevabas . . ." [CXXII] – which recalls the manner of
Soledades, galerías y otros poemas. The hand which guides the

poet through the stylized landscape of the dream – the "mano materna" of earlier poems – is now that of Leonor herself, and the authenticity of the vision seems to qualify the finality of her death. The ending of the poem – "Vive, esperanza : ¡quién sabe/ lo que se traga la tierra!" – is close to that of another, "Dice la esperanza : un día . . ." [CXX], in which the conflict between hope and despair is stated in more abstract terms. And it is these terms – "esperanza" and "amargura" – which Machado attempts to reconcile in the last poem of this group [CXXIV]. If one possible source of reassurance lies in dream, another may be suggested by the sight of natural renewal :

> con este dulce soplo
> que triunfa de la muerte y de la piedra,
> esta amargura que me ahoga fluye
> en esperanza de Ella . . .

What concerns Machado at the moment, however, is not the continuity of life in general, but the grounds for believing in the persistence of a particular life. The most memorable poem of the group seems to rule out any such possibility :

> Señor, ya me arrancaste lo que yo más quería.
> Oye otra vez, Dios mío, mi corazón clamar.
> Tu voluntad se hizo, Señor, contra la mía.
> Señor, ya estamos solos mi corazón y el mar.
>
> [CXIX]*

The "sea" here seems less a symbol of death than of the un-known, as if the death of Leonor meant the loss of any guiding principle in life. Yet what is most striking, in view of Machado's habitual agnosticism, is the actual invocation to God. In a slightly earlier poem, "Profesión de fe" [CXXXVII, v], Machado had begun to sketch out the idea of a God who is not only the creator, but is also in some sense created by the individual. As Aurora de Albornoz has pointed out, several of the concepts of this poem

---

*This seems to be a variant of the uncollected poem which Machado included in his letter to Unamuno of 1913: "Señor, me cansa la vida. / Tengo la garganta ronca / de gritar sobre los mares, / la voz de la mar me asorda. / Señor, me cansa la vida / y el universo me ahoga. / Señor, me dejaste solo, / solo, con el mar a solas."

are influenced by Unamuno, whose notion of a God whose existence would be a natural consequence of the individual's need
for immortality seems to have haunted Machado at this crucial
phase of his life (7, 240). In the poems which refer most directly
to the death of Leonor, the desire to believe in her immortality
leads Machado to consider the possibility of God with even
greater urgency. In "Señor, ya me arrancaste . . .", the appeal is
to a God who has the power both to give and to take away human
happiness. The third line, with its echo of the Lord's Prayer
("Thy will be done . . ."), hovers between protest and acceptance,
only to give way to a sense of total abandonment. Yet not every
poem in the group shares this finality : in several of them, as we
have seen, there is at least a possibility of hope. Clearly, if such
hope is to be more than a delusion, it must be based on an assurance that death is less than a total separation. It is precisely this
assurance which Machado is seeking in the concluding lines of
"Dice la esperanza . . ." and "Soñé que tú me llevabas . . .".
From a strictly Christian standpoint, the God Machado envis-
ages at this stage is inadequate and contradictory, though this in
itself seems a mark of his sincerity. As Aurora de Albornoz puts
it :

Lo mismo que un ortodoxo católico puede hacer sincerísima
poesía religiosa dentro de la más pura ortodoxia, el Machado
de estos años creyó, sin duda, en la necesidad de crear al Dios
productor de inmortalidad. O, por lo menos, creyó en la
necesidad de emprender la búsqueda. Y en esta búsqueda hizo
de Unamuno su guía espiritual (7, 244).

This phase in Machado's verse lasts only a short time : the
effect of this particular aspect of Unamuno's thought begins to
fade after 1913, as he begins to move towards the very different
kind of metaphysical speculations which occupy so much of his
later writing. Inevitably, the loss of his wife and his departure
from Soria continue to affect the poems of this period in many
ways. Only once, however, does Machado write a poem whose
whole nature is determined by the death of Leonor, and it is one
which is completely free from any straining after belief. This is

"A José María Palacio" [CXXVI], one of the finest of his shorter pieces. In it, his characteristic reticence is embodied in the whole structure of what he is saying. The poem takes the form of a verse-letter addressed to one of Machado's friends in Soria.* Soria itself is evoked, rather than described: the more realistic features of the landscape have disappeared, and instead we are given something much more pure: a kind of ideal picture which is created in the imagination, rather than observed.

Again, one notices immediately how the poem is made to echo certain others. This, of course, is one of the characteristics of *Campos de Castilla* as a whole: the fact that Machado's experience centres round a fairly small number of themes and visual impressions. But what we find in this poem seems a deliberate accumulation of these: things which were described more fully in earlier poems are now merely suggested. Some of the same details appear, for instance, in a more elaborate form in "Recuerdos" [CXVI]. And in this poem, written in April, 1913,† there is even a hint of the same grammatical construction:

> ¿Dará sus verdes hojas el olmo aquel del Duero?
> Tendrán los campanarios de Soria sus cigüeñas . . .

This syntactical twist – the question followed by the supposition – becomes the main device in the movement of the other poem:

> ¿Hay zarzas florecidas
> entre las grises peñas,
> y blancas margaritas
> entre la fina hierba?
> Por esos campanarios
> ya habrán ido llegando las cigüeñas.

---

*Carlos Beceiro (*18*) points out that when the poem was first published in *El Porvenir Castellano* (8-v-1916), it was simply dated "Baeza, 29 abril", and that Machado only later added the date "1913". He suggests that the published version may be a revision of an earlier one written three years previously, and adds: "es seguro que . . . Machado *sentía* su poema como de 1913."

†In most editions, this poem is wrongly dated. The correct date is April, 1913, as given in the 1917 edition of *Poesías completas*.

Within this movement, there is an obvious division between
the series of questions which make up the body of the poem –
the questions which evoke the impression of Soria in spring – and
the last four lines, built around the imperative "sube": no longer
tentative, but an urgent request. Both parts are closely connected;
in a sense, it is the first which creates the whole atmosphere
which makes the request possible: "Since it is spring now in
Soria, take the first spring flowers and lay them on my wife's
grave." To say this openly, of course, destroys the whole effect
of the poem. Machado, in fact, never refers to his dead wife by
name; he merely says "al alto Espino donde está su tierra": the
Espino, the cemetery of Soria, is now her "land", almost as if
he were referring to a living person.

The first part of the poem carefully builds up the feeling that
spring is a period of suspense; what Machado is thinking of is
the precise moment at which spring begins first to appear, when
the first signs of spring coincide with the last traces of winter.
One remembers, of course, that spring in the north-east of Spain
comes later than in the south: in Andalusia, where Machado is
writing, spring would have come before this (in Soria, it is only
just beginning), and the fact gives a special poignancy to what
he is imagining. One notices also how careful he is to distin-
guish between the signs of spring and those of winter:

> ¿Tienen los viejos olmos
> algunas hojas nuevas?
> Aún las acacias estarán desnudas
> y nevados los montes de las sierras,

or, more economically still:

> ¿Hay ciruelos en flor? ¿Quedan violetas?

With such touches in mind, we might say that the essential tone
of the poem was one of possibility. Machado is not describing the
various manifestations of spring; they are all things which he
feels to be imminent. And in asking his friend whether spring in
Soria is already a reality, he is drawing on his memory of other
springs. That is to say, as in "A un olmo seco", time – past,
present and future – plays an important part in the poem. The

past corresponds to the poet's own memories; the present is
Machado writing his poem in an Andalusian town; the future
is the realm of possibility which he conceives in his questions.
(Also, when one looks back over the whole poem, there are
hints of a further idea which binds together all three stages of
time : the thought that, as Ricardo Gullón puts it, "primavera
y hermosura ya no son para Leonor" (*10*, 125).)

If one tries to analyse the emotional overtones of the first part
of the poem, one thinks inevitably in terms of Machado's attitude to Soria. Clearly, this is one of Machado's most affectionate
poems, one in which his feeling for Soria is made even stronger
by absence. Perhaps one can go further than this, and say that a
kind of emotional shift takes place, by which some of his feelings for his dead wife are transferred to the place itself. And if
this were true, it would seem to reinforce the hesitant note of
the questioning, almost, as Carlos Beceiro says, as if a timid lover
were asking a friend for news of the woman he loves (*17*, 137).

The second part of the poem – the last four lines – breaks abruptly into this mood of hesitation. What is suggested here,
rather than a Soria which is merely sketched-in by the memory,
is a real town, the town where Machado's friend actually is at
the moment of writing, made even more immediate by the use of
the place-name, "el alto Espino". Thus the concreteness of the
ending raises the poem to a point of dramatic tension in which
Machado's real wish – his motive for addressing his friend in
the first place – suddenly breaks through the carefully built-up
atmosphere of the first part. And, ultimately, the subtlety of the
poem lies in the way each part complements and qualifies the
other; as Sánchez Barbudo observes :

> Es la muerte de Leonor lo que hace para él remota, inalcan-
> zable, esa primavera que añora; pero a su vez ese nuevo florecer
> soriano que imagina envuelve su dolor, haciéndolo más ligero,
> más contenido (*13*, 265).

Hardly surprisingly, Machado's first feelings on settling in Baeza seem to have been of sterility and alienation in the midst of a landscape which, paradoxically, was more native to him than that of Soria. The earliest indication of this mood occurs in what must be one of the first poems written after the death of Leonor, "A Xavier Valcarce" [CXLI], originally published in January, 1913:

> No sé, Valcarce, mas cantar no puedo;
> se ha dormido la voz en mi garganta,
> y tiene el corazón un salmo quedo.
> Ya sólo reza el corazón, no canta.

Its fullest expression, however, comes in a much finer poem, "En estos campos de la tierra mía . . ." [CXXV], dated 4th April, 1913. Here, though there is no mention of Leonor, the polarity between Soria and Andalusia dominates the poem from the beginning:

> En estos campos de la tierra mía,
> y extranjero en los campos de mi tierra
> – yo tuve patria donde corre el Duero . . .

For once, the reasons for Machado's attachment to Soria are implied, rather than stated: his immediate problem is to find the means of continuing to write poetry in a "native country" – Andalusia – which is no longer his "true home". In what follows, the comparison is not between Machado's memories of Soria and the reality of his present surroundings, but between two sets of mental images. The reason for this is clear: if the present is alien, there may still be material for poetry in his memories of the distant past. This is precisely what the rest of the poem denies. Several of the images Machado recalls – notably "el limonero/de ramas polvorientas" – are ones which occur in *Soledades, galerías y otros poemas*; they are images, in other words, once felt to be meaningful. Yet, because of the experience which has come between, they have lost their power to compel: they are no longer true memories, but "despojos del recuerdo", a patchwork of discordant colours. The crucial lines come just before this:

> mas falta el hilo que el recuerdo anuda
> al corazón, el ancla en su ribera,
> o estas memorias no son alma ...*

What is lacking is the thread of emotion which would make them live in the poet's imagination at the present time, and it is this which distinguishes them from the memories of Soria. The last two lines, however, suggest that this may not always be so:

> Un día tornarán, con luz del fondo ungidos,
> los cuerpos virginales a la orilla vieja.

Sánchez Barbudo regards this ending as weak:

> Lo de volver "con luz del fondo ungidos", da a esos cuerpos – que no se sabe exactamente qué cuerpos sean – un aire espectral; y la esperanza queda así pospuesta hasta el día del Juicio Final, poco más o menos (*13*, 264).

My own reading is rather different: the "cuerpos virginales", I would suggest, are the memories themselves – an extension of the body metaphor already implied in "sus abigarradas vestimentas". It is as if Machado were saying: "At some time in the future, these memories of Andalusia, which are now like bodies clothed in meaningless colours, will return in their original, unspoiled form." The actual pattern of metaphor is, in fact, richer than this, though perfectly coherent. In the last line, "la orilla vieja" takes up "ribera [del corazón]": the memories will one day return to the shore – the heart – to which they were once "anchored" in the past. And they will return "con luz del fondo ungidos", illuminated, in unbroken continuity, from the depths of the poet's own mind.

---

*Glendinning (*21*, 69) notes a similar use of "un fil" in Bergson. Compare also the line in Machado's poem to Narciso Alonso Cortés [CXLIX]: "Poeta, el alma sólo es ancla en la ribera."

Perhaps no other poem of *Campos de Castilla* shows more clearly than this one Machado's powers of self-judgement and his ability to make fine poetry out of unpromising circumstances. At the same time, one should not take his complaints of sterility too literally. In the early part of 1913, he had already written poems as accomplished as "Recuerdos" [CXVI] and "Del pasado efímero" [CXXXI], as well as, to all appearances, the magnificent "Poema de un día" [CXXVIII], which I shall discuss in the next section. What is certain is that the mood of isolation so movingly suggested in "En estos campos de la tierra mía . . ." runs like a ground-note through the poems of the next few years. Sometimes, as in "Poema de un día", the memory of Leonor is no more than a thought which crosses the poet's mind as he listens to the ticking of the clock :

> . . . Era un día
> (tic-tic, tic-tic . . .) que pasó,
> y lo que yo más quería
> la muerte se lo llevó.

At others, it is a wound which threatens to destroy his whole sense of identity :

> Tan pobre me estoy quedando,
> que ya ni siquiera estoy
> conmigo, ni sé si voy
> conmigo a solas viajando.

[CXXVII]

One of the things which sustained Machado through these difficult years was his friendship with Unamuno : not only his admiration for the trenchancy of the other writer's approach to questions of belief, but also the sense of sharing common ground with a fellow-dissident. In the letter of 1913 from which I have already quoted, he describes to Unamuno the atmosphere of Baeza :

Esta Baeza, que llaman Salamanca andaluza, tiene un Instituto, un Seminario, una Escuela de Artes, varios colegios de segunda enseñanza, y apenas sabe leer un 30 por ciento de la población. No hay más que una librería donde se venden tarjetas postales, devocionarios y periódicos clericales y pornográficos. Es la comarca más rica de Jaén y la ciudad está poblada de mendigos y de señoritos arruinados en la ruleta. La profesión de jugador de monte se considera muy honroso. Es infinitamente más levítica y no hay un átomo de religiosidad. Se habla de política – todo el mundo es conservador – y se discute con pasión cuando la Audiencia de Jaén viene a celebrar algún juicio por jurados . . . Por lo demás, el hombre del campo trabaja y sufre resignado o emigra en condiciones tan lamentables que equivalen al suicidio.

As for writing, he concludes:

Cuando se vive en estos páramos espirituales, no se puede escribir nada suave, porque necesita uno la indignación para no helarse también. (3, 164–5).

In the poems of these years, Machado's indignation takes many forms. The range of his satirical writing is as impressive in its way as that of the more reflective Soria poems. It runs from the gentleness of parts of "Poema de un día" to the corrosive denunciation of "El mañana efímero" [CXXXV] and "Una España joven" [CXLIV], though it is never better than when he relies on his quite remarkable powers of direct observation. Two poems, in particular, are close to the spirit, and occasionally to the details, of the letter to Unamuno: "Del pasado efímero" [CXXXI] – originally entitled "Hombres de España (Del pasado superfluo)" – and "Llanto de las virtudes y coplas por la muerte de Don Guido" [CXXXIII]. The first of these, published in March, 1913, is a pointed description of a recognizable provincial figure: the small-time farmer whose horizons are limited by gambling, local politics and his memories of sensational events in the past.* The richness of the detail – the accuracy of the vocabulary is one of the poem's great strengths – scarcely conceals Machado's contempt, which breaks out in the final reflection:

---

*The reference in the second line is to a famous bullfighter of the 1880s, José Sánchez del Campo, *Cara-Ancha*, who revived the technique of killing the bull by "receiving" it, i.e. by utilizing the actual force of the bull's charge. He first performed this feat on 19th June, 1881, which gives a certain precision to the "un día" of the poem.

> Este hombre no es de ayer ni es de mañana,
> sino de nunca; de la cepa hispana
> no es el fruto maduro ni podrido,
> es una fruta vana
> de aquella España que pasó y no ha sido,
> esa que hoy tiene la cabeza cana.

This is no mere rhetorical outburst: the terms of the condemnation are precisely chosen and the gap which divides his subject from any meaningful tradition is carefully plotted. The "España que pasó y no ha sido" is not simply an anachronism: it is an invention of those who are trapped in a totally unreal present.

The second poem is more complex, if only because of its literary echoes. As far as the subject is concerned, it is likely that Don Guido was based on a real-life model, though Machado may have also remembered an essay of Unamuno's in which he explains the character of Don Juan in terms of *señoritismo*:

> ... después de pasados los años de su ardiente mocedad, suele casarse y se convierte en un respetable burgués, lleno de achaques y de prejuicios, conservador y hasta neo. Oye misa diaria, pertenece a varias cofradías y abomina de cuantos no respetan las venerables tradiciones de nuestros mayores (quoted 7, 197).*

The resemblance to the "plot" of Machado's poem is striking, though hardly conclusive, since both authors are describing a familiar type. What is certain is the way the title alludes to one of the most famous poems in the language: the *Coplas por la muerte de su padre* of the fifteenth-century poet Jorge Manrique. It is clear that Machado greatly admired this poem, to which he refers at several points in his work. In the present context, the effect is obviously parodic: in suggesting the title, and occasionally the actual rhythms, of Manrique's elegy, Machado is setting an ironical distance, not only between himself and Don Guido, but also, one might argue, between the latter and Manrique's own subject, the truly aristocratic Maestre de Santiago. Yet, despite such echoes, the "Llanto" is far from being a "literary" poem, and one of the things which saves it from this is the skill

---

*Unamuno, *Obras completas*, ed. cit., IV, 487.

with which Machado hints at another, quite unliterary, kind of poetry: that of the popular *aleluyas*.* This comes out, above all, in the clipped rhythms and the deliberately insistent rhyming:

> Hoy nos dice la campana
> que han de llevarse mañana
> al buen don Guido, muy serio,
> camino del cementerio.

As might be expected, Machado is not content with mere imitation: lines like these make their effect by taking the laconic clichés of the *aleluyas* and raising them to the level of genuine wit. At the same time, the playfulness of the tone and the general air of burlesque should not blind one to the essential seriousness of the poem. Like the "hombre del casino provinciano" of the previous poem, Don Guido is a "hollow man", the embodiment of a false respectability devoid of any real spiritual values. Hence the finality of his death; as Machado wrote in an article of 1915:

> Yo creo que sólo mueren definitivamente – perdonadme esta fe un tanto herética – sin salvación posible, los malvados y los farsantes, esos hombres de presa que llamamos caciques, esos repugnantes cucañistas que se dicen políticos, los histriones de todos los escenarios, los fariseos de todos los cultos . . .†

The article in which this sentence occurs is a tribute to Francisco Giner de los Ríos, the founder of the Institución Libre de Enseñanza, who died on 18th February, 1915.‡ Both the prose piece and the poem which immediately followed it [CXXXIX] express very strikingly the positive values which Machado felt to be embodied in his former teacher, and, in doing so, make clear the moral basis of his satire. The exemplary nature of Giner is stressed at every point:

---

*The *aleluyas* were religious in origin, but from the 18th century onwards were adapted to a great variety of purposes: satirical, didactic and burlesque. In their most popular form, they consist of a story told in picture-frames, each of which is accompanied by a rhyming couplet. For more details, see J. Caro Baroja, *Ensayo sobre la literatura de cordel* (Madrid, 1969), 409–30.

†The article is reproduced by Jorge Campos in "Antonio Machado y Giner de los Ríos (comentario a un texto olvidado)", *La Torre*, XII, 45–6 (1964), 59–64.

‡Machado's article appeared in the Baeza magazine *Idea Nueva* on 23rd February, 1915; the poem was published in *España* three days later.

Como todos los grandes andaluces, era D. Francisco la viva antí-
tesis del andaluz de pandereta, del andaluz mueble, jactancioso,
hiperbolizante y amigo de lo que brilla y de lo que truena.
Carecía de vanidades, pero no de orgullo; convencido de ser,
desdeñaba el aparentar. Era sencillo, austero hasta la santidad,
amigo de las proporciones justas y de las medidas cabales. Era
un místico, pero no contemplativo y extático, sino laborioso y
activo. Tenía el alma fundadora de Teresa de Avila y de Iñigo
de Loyola; pero él se adueñaba de los espíritus por la libertad
y por el amor.

The slow metre of the poem could hardly be more different from
the leaping rhythms of the "Llanto": unlike Don Guido, Giner
is a man whose death is in no sense an extinction. Much of the
poem's strength comes, in fact, from the avoidance of conventional elegy. Giner's legacy is conveyed, not by posthumous
praise, but in the tones of his own voice, a living voice which
expressly forbids mourning. In its simplest terms, it is a lesson in
virtue:

> Sed buenos y no más, sed lo que he sido
> entre vosotros: alma.

As in other poems of Machado's, it is a virtue which leads to
right action; as he says in "Proverbios y cantares" [CXXXVI,
xi] : "Virtud es fortaleza, ser bueno es ser valiente." One notices
also the absence of Christian overtones: the "otra luz más pura"
is hardly more than a poetic fiction; what matters is "el sol de los
talleres", the light of every day which shines on a strictly human
activity. (The phrase "enmudeced, campanas" also seems to reject a specifically Christian symbol.)

In endorsing Giner's hopes for a "new Spain", Machado is
confirming his own preoccupation with the question of national
renewal. The roots of this concern, of course, go back a long
way;* at the same time, there is no doubt that Machado's determination to face up to the social and political realities of Spanish

---

*In his essay of 1908, "Nuestro patriotismo y la marcha de Cádiz" (4, I,
85–7), Machado wrote: "Por lo pronto, nuestro patriotismo ha cambiado
de rumbo y de cauce. Sabemos ya que no se puede vivir ni del esfuerzo, ni
de la virtud, ni de la fortuna de nuestros abuelos ... Luchamos por libertarnos
del culto supersticioso del pasado."

life intensified in the course of the Baeza period. There are times, indeed, when it seems like an act of self-preservation; shortly after his wife's death, he wrote to Juan Ramón Jiménez :

> Cuando perdí a mi mujer, pensé pegarme un tiro. El éxito de mi libro [i.e. *Campos de Castilla*] me salvó, y no por vanidad, ¡bien lo sabe Dios!, sino porque pensé que, si había en mí una fuerza útil, no tenía derecho a aniquilarla. Quiero trabajar, humildemente, es cierto, pero con eficacia, con verdad. Hay que defender la España que surge, del mar muerto, de la España inerte y abrumadora que amenaza anegarlo todo (quoted *14*, 80).

Though Machado's poems and correspondence of this period show an acute awareness of current events and attitudes, it would be a mistake to look for a coherent political philosophy in them. It is Machado's honesty, rather than his consistency, which is impressive : the presence of a distinctive voice which is not afraid to commit itself on issues to which there is no simple solution. Nevertheless, it is possible to see certain tendencies or ideas which affect Machado's approach to such issues. In the first place, he is aware that a number of younger writers – among them Pérez de Ayala and Ortega y Gasset – are begining to make a reputation, writers who, on the whole, are more disciplined intellectually than those of the previous generation.*
This is the tone of the short poem [CXL] which Machado dedicated to Ortega in 1915, in which the strict architecture of new modes of thought is connected, perhaps a little obscurely, with the Protestant austerity of German philosophy. Ortega, in fact, was the first editor of *España*, the new liberal review founded in 1915, to which Machado contributed several poems, including the ode to Giner. The common aim which such a magazine represented – roughly speaking, the wish to educate the country as a whole through the work of an informed minority – was clearly sympathetic to Machado, though it is doubtful whether he would have accepted some of its more élitist implications. At the least, however, it seems to have confirmed his growing belief

---

*Pérez de Ayala published his fourth novel, *Troteras y danzaderas*, in 1913, and not long afterwards became known as a writer on theatre and politics. Ortega's first book, *Meditaciones del Quijote*, appeared in 1914.

in the social rôle of the poet, in its way a new version of the "objectivity" for which he had been striving a few years previously. The sense that a new cultural situation was emerging also sharpened his attitude towards those of his own contemporaries who appeared to have abandoned the struggle. This explains, among other things, the criticism of Azorín implied in the ending of "Desde mi rincón" [CXLIII].* Though the poem as a whole is uneven, Machado's tribute is scarcely conventional, and the closing lines break out with some force from the rest:

> ¡Oh tú, *Azorín*, escucha : España quiere
> surgir, brotar, toda una España empieza!
> ¿Y ha de helarse en la España que se muere?
> ¿Ha de ahogarse en la España que bosteza?
> Para salvar la nueva epifanía
> hay que acudir, ya es hora,
> con el hacha y el fuego al nuevo día.
> Oye cantar los gallos de la aurora.

Machado is obviously moved by Azorín's evocation of a timeless Spain, yet he clearly does not see how such a vision can lead to the future Spain in which he himself believes. Azorín's aesthetic rendering of the past not only fails to allow for the possibility of change; it excludes the kind of reality which Machado sees around him as he writes, the "pueblo que ayuna y se divierte,/ora y eructa . . .". For Machado, the real test of faith is to believe in the future while taking the full measure of the present, and his concluding lines are an invitation to the "reactionary" Azorín to join in bringing this future about.

This call to action points to a second feature of Machado's writings of this period : the revolutionary streak which he refers to on several occasions, usually with a certain sense of pride. Towards the end of this particular poem he exclaims:

> ¡admirable *Azorín*, el reaccionario
> por asco de la greña jacobina! –;

---

*Machado seems to have been dissatisfied with this poem. In a letter of 1913 to Juan Ramón Jiménez he wrote: "Acaso encuentres en esa composición alguna crudeza . . . Hay un cierto desgarramiento inevitable e impurezas que mi espíritu arrastra cuando se desborda y superficializa" (4, II, 86).

and in an earlier poem, "Retrato" [XCVII], he confesses: "Hay en mis venas gotas de sangre jacobina . . .". This last remark may simply be an allusion to certain nineteenth-century ancestors: to his liberal and anti-clerical grandfather, Antonio Machado Núñez, or to his remarkable great-grandfather, Juan Alvarez Guerra, the author of a philosophical treatise entitled *Unidad simbólica y destino del hombre en la tierra, o filosofía de la razón por un amigo del hombre* (4 vols., 1837–57).* What is interesting, however, is the persistent use of the word "jacobino", with its conscious reference to the French revolutionary tradition. The sense that this was also in some way a family tradition is borne out by a curious passage in a letter to Unamuno written on 16th 'January, 1915. Speaking of his growing sympathy for the French cause in the Great War, Machado attacks what he calls "la Francia reaccionaria": the right-wing tradition of Action Française. He goes on:

> . . . la otra Francia es de mi familia y aun de mi casa, es la de mi padre y de mi abuelo y de mi bisabuelo; que todos pasaron la frontera y amaron la Francia de la libertad y del laicismo, la Francia religiosa del *affaire* [Dreyfus] y de la Separación de Roma, en nuestros días. Y ésa será la que triunfe, si triunfa, de Alemania (*3, 172*).

Thus Machado's radicalism, like so much else in his life, is more a matter of temperament and personal conviction than of belief in an existing programme. This, unfortunately, makes it difficult to estimate the kind of positive action he calls for in certain poems of the time. His concern with political events – the split between the liberal parties and the Church, the growing power of popular left-wing movements – is clear enough, and he makes no attempt to conceal his republican sympathies. Yet in the poems themselves, the cry for reform is seldom more than a vague threat:

> Mas otra España nace,
> la España del cincel y de la maza,
> con esa eterna juventud que se hace

---

*On the curious parallels between this work and Machado's *Abel Martín*, see José María Valverde, *5*, 48–50.

del pasado macizo de la raza.
Una España implacable y redentora,
España que alborea
con un hacha en la mano vengadora,
España de la rabia y de la idea.

[CXXV]

These lines, from the end of "El mañana efímero", contrast
strongly with the gentler optimism of the poem to Giner, written
two years later. The aggressiveness of certain images probably
owes something to Unamuno, though the voice is unmistakably
Machado's.* As Sánchez Barbudo observes: "Como otras veces
en los poemas de esta época, Machado profetiza, y parece desear,
una violenta revolución" (*13*, 302). As to what such a revolution
might entail, Machado is never explicit: the desire for a clean
sweep, at whatever cost, is explained – though perhaps not entirely justified – by the exasperation expressed in the earlier part
of the poem. This exasperation is not as uncontrolled as some
critics have thought. The lines which are most often quoted –

Esa España inferior que ora y bosteza,
vieja y tahur, zaragatera y triste;
esa España inferior que ora y embiste
cuando se digna usar de la cabeza . . .

– are not the denunciation of religion they are sometimes taken
to be.† What Machado is attacking is not "la España que ora",
but "la España que ora y bosteza", the Spain for which religion
has ceased to be a living reality. And, since he sees no easy solution to this – "aun tendrá luengo parto de varones . . ." –, it is
perhaps understandable that he should go on to identify ven-
geance with redemption.

*Ribbans (*12*, 303) notes Machado's liking for the word "maza" in this
type of context, particularly when he is addressing Unamuno. Compare the
lines from "A Don Miguel de Unamuno" [CLI], written in 1905: "Y el
alma desalmada de su raza, / que bajo el golpe de su férrea maza / aún
duerme, puede que despierte un día."
†Laín Entralgo considers Machado's picture of Spain in this poem
"brutal e injusto" and describes the lines which I quote as "cuatro de los
más atroces versos que jamás se hayan escrito sobre la realidad de la vida
española" (*La generación del noventa y ocho*, Madrid, 1945, 182).

This brings us to a third factor, which I have already touched on : Machado's anti-clericalism. Though in a sense this is a basic part of the liberal tradition to which he belongs, it is complicated at this stage by the search for genuine religious values which is a striking feature of his correspondence with Unamuno. Machado makes no secret of his contempt for organized religion; on the other hand, the growing concern with society which one finds in the writings of the Baeza period leads him to reflect at times on the Christian ideal of brotherhood. As I have tried to show, Machado's interest in religious belief quickens very noticeably at the time of his wife's death in 1912. Understandably, this takes the form of a wish to believe in the possibility of immortality, which in turn is influenced by Unamuno's notion of a God who is created out of man's own necessities. This, basically, is the God Machado refers to in "Desde mi rincón", where he speaks of

> . . . una fe que nace
> cuando se busca a Dios y no se alcanza,
> y en el Dios que se lleva y que se hace.

Nevertheless, this particular idea seems to have had less importance for Machado after 1913, and is eventually replaced by a quite different and still less orthodox concept of God, the "Gran Ser que hizo la Nada" of *Juan de Mairena* and the other prose writings. This later development is scarcely foreshadowed at the time of *Campos de Castilla*; what is immediately relevant is the kind of importance Machado attaches to the figure of Christ.

As early as 1909, he had written :

> ¿Para qué llamar caminos
> a los surcos del azar? . . .
> Todo el que camina anda,
> como Jesús, sobre el mar.

[CXXXVI, ii]

As Aurora de Albornoz comments :

> No es el crucificado, el agonizante, el que va a morir, el que a Machado le interesa : es el vivo. Un Jesús vivo, capaz de dominar el mar (7, 261).

This is equally true of the later writings: at the time of the
Baeza poems, and for long afterwards, Christ is for Machado the
supreme symbol of human brotherhood. Writing to Unamuno
on 16th January, 1918, a year after the second version of *Campos
de Castilla*, he says:

> Si dijéramos que [la fraternidad] es el amor al prójimo por
> amor de nosotros mismos, no interpretaríamos, a mi juicio, el
> espíritu cristiano; sería entonces la fraternidad una forma in-
> directa de amarse cada cual a sí mismo. Me parece, más bien,
> la fraternidad el amor al prójimo por amor al padre común . . .
> Tal me parece a mí el sentido del Evangelio y la gran reve-
> lación del Cristo, el verdadero transmutador de valores. La
> humildad es un sentimiento cristiano, porque el amor que
> Cristo ordena es un amor sin orgullo, sin deleite en nosotros
> ni en nuestra obra; nosotros no podríamos engendrar el objeto
> de nuestro amor, a nuestro hermano, obra de Dios. El amor
> fraternal nos saca de nuestra soledad y nos lleva a Dios. Cuando
> reconozco que hay otro yo, que no soy yo mismo ni es obra
> mía, caigo en la cuenta de que Dios existe y que debo de creer
> en él como en un padre (*3*, 178–9).

It seems characteristic of Machado that he should think of Christ
as a means of access to God, rather than simply as God made
man. It is also significant that he never attempts to define the
idea of a "padre común": any Christian overtones which remain in his notion of God soon disappear, as I have suggested,
in the metaphysical abstractions of *Juan de Mairena*. What continues to attract him is the figure of Christ as a symbol of true
fraternity, the natural antithesis to the Cain of the earlier poems,
a conception which perhaps owes as much to Tolstoy as to
Unamuno.* This division which seems to have existed in
Machado's mind between God and Christ can be detected in
certain poems of "Proverbios y cantares". Here, God is almost
invariably associated with sleep or dreams:

---

*In the letter to Unamuno just quoted, Machado writes: "Sólo los rusos
—¡bendito pueblo!—me parecen capaces de superarlo [i.e. el patriotismo]
por un sentimiento más noble y universal. El tolstoismo salvará a Europa,
si es que ésta tiene salvación" (*3*, 178).

Ayer soñé que veía
a Dios y que a Dios hablaba; . . .

[CXXXVI, xxi]

and again :

Todo hombre tiene dos
batallas que pelear :
en sueños lucha con Dios;
y despierto, con el mar.

[do., xxviii]

Christ, on the other hand, is seen in terms of vigilance :

Yo amo a Jesús, que nos dijo :
Cielo y tierra pasarán.
Cuando cielo y tierra pasen
mi palabra quedará.
¿Cuál fue, Jesús, tu palabra?
¿Amor? ¿Perdón? ¿Caridad?
Todas tus palabras fueron
una palabra : Velad.

[do., xxxiv]

This, in other words, is the positive side to Machado's anti-
clericalism : the belief, for a time at least, in the possibility of a
God whose nature is denied by official religion, and the more
enduring sense of Christ as the essential touchstone for social
action. Like the other ideas I have discussed in this section, these
seldom appear directly in the actual poems of the Baeza period.
Yet some such understanding of Machado's attitudes at this stage
seems essential if we are to do justice to those poems which, on
the face of it, may seem merely destructive or over-rhetorical.
Whether he is commenting on Spain's neutrality in the Great
War ("España en paz", CXLV), or on the failure of the Moder-
nist dream ("Una España joven", CXLIV), one admires the
sense of responsibility and the self-awareness with which he is
prepared to speak on living issues, even when the results are un-
satisfactory as poems. Above all, perhaps, it was in the Baeza
period that Machado began to develop the habit of intense reflection on every conceivable aspect of his circumstances which
he continued to exercise until the end of his life.

A good deal of Machado's thinking, as we have seen, was directed at his fellow-countrymen; as Tuñón de Lara has said:

> . . . es precisamente en estos años [que] se produce en Machado ese enriquecimiento de su personalidad creadora en diferentes proyecciones, en un plano más elevado y con un sentido de su responsabilidad hacia el prójimo, hacia los *otros* . . . (*14*, 92).

Nevertheless, it would be wrong to suppose that Machado had deliberately turned himself into a public poet; his preoccupation with religious belief alone would suggest otherwise, and the kind of self-examination this entails can also be seen in the number of poems and aphorisms in which he speculates on philosophical issues. Machado's interest in such matters dates back at least as far as 1909, when he published the first twenty of the "Proverbios y cantares".* In 1911, he attended the lectures of the philosopher Henri Bergson in Paris, and it is clear that Bergson's views on the nature of time and flux helped him to formulate the views on the function of poetry which are expressed in his later prose works. A few years later, at the age of forty, he enrolled for philosophy classes at the University of Madrid; as he wrote to Federico de Onís in 1932:

> Mis estudios de Filosofía, en Madrid, han sido muy tardíos . . . La necesidad de un título académico fue, en verdad, el pretexto para consagrar unos cuantos años a una afición de toda mi vida (quoted *14*, 99–100).

To see the full consequences of Machado's philosophical studies would take us far beyond the period of *Campos de Castilla*. Nevertheless, one can make certain generalizations which may help to explain some of the more cryptic poems of this

---

*Of the others, nos. xlii–l were published in *La Lectura* in 1913 and no. xxviii in 1916. The rest appeared for the first time in the 1917 edition of *Poesías completas*.

phase and to show how they relate to other aspects of his work. In the first place, though he is clearly fascinated by certain philosophical problems, Machado never writes as a professional philosopher. This is not a question of training, but of temperament: as a poet, he mistrusts any kind of knowledge which deals in concepts and abstractions. Secondly, many of his observations, especially in "Proverbios y cantares", are deliberately cast in a popular form. This, one might argue, is another attempt at "objective" writing: by adopting the manner of the popular proverb, or of earlier moralists,* Machado is creating an effect of anonymity which to some extent distances his more personal reflections. And in the "Parábolas", the fable technique seems to anticipate the "apocryphal" writings of *Abel Martín* and *Juan de Mairena*, in which invented situations and attitudes are part of the essential irony. Finally, this type of writing is not as remote from the other poems as it might seem. The "Proverbios y cantares" are not the homogeneous block they appear to be in the collected editions, but were written over a period of seven or eight years. As Gutiérrez-Girardot points out:

> . . . su ordenación no parece obedecer a un hilo consecuente, aunque vistos más de cerca, se muestran como variaciones, aproximaciones, repeticiones y, a grandes rasgos, como uno más entre los múltiples resúmenes de la poesía de Machado (*11*, 41).

A list of their themes would correspond very closely to those we have already seen in other poems of the period, and quite often Machado seems to be probing the implications of certain images which he has already used more or less intuitively.

This last point can be illustrated first, since it involves a number of poems which are not strictly philosophical. No. xxix of "Proverbios y cantares", for example, reads:

> Caminante, son tus huellas
> el camino, y nada más;
> caminante, no hay camino,
> se hace camino al andar.

*Various critics have detected the influence of the fourteenth-century poet Santob de Carrión, author of the *Proverbios morales*, whom Machado mentions by name in *Nuevas canciones* ("Proverbios y cantares", CLXI, lxi).

> Al andar se hace camino,
> y al volver la vista atrás
> se ve la senda que nunca
> se ha de volver a pisar.
> Caminante, no hay camino,
> sino estelas en la mar.

The road as a metaphor of life is, of course, one of Machado's commonest images, and occurs in some of his earliest poems. The sea is also a favourite image, though it appears rather later in his verse, and fluctuates between several meanings: chaos, the unknown (as here) and death. Both images are traditional, as are the form and general tone of the poem. What is distinctive, on the other hand, is the way Machado has brought the two images together to form a paradox. Logically, the poem moves through a chain of affirmations and negations: there is no road but the traveller's own footprints: the traveller *is* the "road"; yet, unlike a real road, this one allows of no turning back. But in the last two lines, the metaphor is changed: the illusion of a "path" which the traveller leaves behind is destroyed in its turn; there are, after all, no footprints, only the wake of the sea which closes behind one as one goes. There are other possible overtones – Christ as the road ("I am the Way . . ."), Christ walking on the waves –, though none of these affects the basic movement of the poem. What survives is the sense that, by sheer force of compression – by bringing together two of his central images in the space of ten lines – Machado has implied with great force something which is only hinted at in his more extended poems: the idea of life as a journeying towards a goal which, though not strictly infinite, always remains distant. Like the experience it attempts to define, such a poem is necessarily open-ended. Machado, in fact, returns to the theme at several points in "Proverbios y cantares", almost always with a shift of emphasis. The most succinct example – and also the most "popular" in tone – is no. xliv:

> Todo pasa y todo queda,
> pero lo nuestro es pasar,
> pasar haciendo caminos,
> caminos sobre la mar.

This retains the road-sea parallel of the previous poem, but modifies it by introducing the thought of death: all things return, except the individual life. And in the poem which immediately follows this [xlv], death becomes the focal point of the meditation:

> Morir . . . ¿Caer como gota
> de mar en el mar inmenso?
> ¿O ser lo que nunca he sido:
> uno, sin sombra y sin sueño,
> un solitario que avanza
> sin camino y sin espejo?

Of the two possibilities Machado entertains, only the first involves the sea, which is now not so much a symbol of the unknown as of total extinction. The third and fourth lines reflect, with marvellous economy, on his whole activity as a poet: what will be abolished is precisely the sense of self-division and the need for a sustaining illusion which have been the driving-force in his work. The closing lines develop the ideal situation by completely detaching the idea of "journeying forward" from the image of the "road", as if the latter belonged only to life. But, at the same time, Machado introduces a new image, though one which is familiar from earlier poems: the mirror which stands for introspection and the memories of the past. And this, in turn, is taken up again in no. xlix, where death is implied in the poet's sense of growing old; age now strips the quicksilver from the mirror – the illusions of his own creating –, so that what once reflected becomes transparent.*

To analyse several of these poems consecutively, as I have just done, may make the process of association seem more deliberate than it actually was. The most remarkable aspect of "Proverbios y cantares" has nothing to do with systematic elaboration: it is quite simply the impression they give of a poet who, at any moment, is capable of reflecting incisively, and often movingly, on the central themes and images of his work. Understandably,

---

*Compare the lines from "Me dijo un alba de la primavera . . ." [XXXIV], originally published in *Soledades:* "Respondí a la mañana: / Sólo tienen cristal los sueños míos."

the nature and quality of Machado's reflections vary a great deal : the observations on human behaviour are sometimes disappointingly obvious and those on national character are scarcely more than footnotes to the longer poems. The best, on the other hand, are those which involve some kind of self-questioning, however much this is concealed by humour or irony. It is this aspect which Machado himself singled out in a note of 1916 :

> Todos creerán que mis epigramas están escritos contra alguien . . . Nadie comprenderá que estos epigramas están escritos contra mí mismo (*3, 35*).

In the later poems of "Proverbios y cantares" and in several of the "Parábolas", this inner debate makes increasing use of philosophical terms, though, paradoxically, in a way which tends to reinforce Machado's mistrust of professional philosophers. At the same time, the fact that Machado does not reject philosophy out of hand may seem contradictory, a state of affairs which is described very well by José María Valverde :

> . . . por lo que toca a la filosofía misma, en aquella época – alrededor de 1915 – Antonio Machado había adquirido ya sus dos convicciones básicas, a primera vista en posible conflicto entre sí : una, bergsoniana, que el pensamiento abstracto no capta la realidad viva, por lo cual la filosofía es siempre un fracaso; otra que – a pesar de su invalidez básica – la filosofía, en ese momento histórico, está expresando muy bien la tendencia general de la cultura, o sea, la esperanza de salir del turbio irracionalismo y del narcisista individualismo del siglo XIX, para volver a ser – como en su mejor momento prístino en Grecia – contemplación de esencias, iluminada visión de la realidad del mundo, de las cosas y de los hombres, en la aurora de una fraternidad universal (*5, 56*).

It is only after *Campos de Castilla* that Machado succeeds in resolving this apparent contradiction, though he does it in a deliberately ambiguous way : by inventing a series of fictitious personages – notably the philosopher-poet Abel Martín and his disciple, Juan de Mairena – whose theories and reflections, though in one sense a product of his own mind, are presented ironically, as if independent of their real author. In the meantime, Machado continues to reflect on his anti-philosophical position in his own person. Occasionally in "Proverbios y cantares" he separates "truth" quite starkly from "thought" or "knowledge" in the analytical sense. Thus, in no. xxx, he is able to say:

> La verdad es lo que es,
> y sigue siendo verdad
> aunque se piense al revés.

and, in the following poem:

> Confiemos
> en que no será verdad
> nada de lo que sabemos.*

Generally, however, the conflict between logic and intuition is presented in metaphorical terms, as in no. xxxv:

> Hay dos modos de conciencia:
> una es luz, y otra, paciencia.
> Una estriba en alumbrar
> un poquito el hondo mar;
> otra, en hacer penitencia
> con caña o red, y esperar
> el pez, como pescador.
> Dime tú: ¿cuál es mejor?
> ¿Conciencia de visionario
> que mira en el hondo acuario
> peces vivos
> fugitivos,
> que no se pueden pescar,
> o esa maldita faena
> de ir arrojando a la arena,
> muertos, los peces del mar?

The point here is that the analytical approach destroys the very reality it seeks to explain by taking it out of its natural element, which is time and flux. What begins as "paciencia" ends as a "maldita faena", unlike the visionary consciousness – the poet's – which perceives things in their true condition. Machado uses the same fishing imagery in two of the "Parábolas". The first of

*A slightly different version of these lines appears in *Abel Martín:* "Confiamos / en que no será verdad / nada de lo que pensamos" (5, 209).

these [ii] is oddly diffuse, and the full meaning of the fable is a little hard to grasp. Yet it is clear that, of the two figures – the dreamer and the thinker – it is the former who is welcomed by the inhabitants of the sea, whereas the latter's thoughts lead to sterility and death:

> Y piensa : "Es esta vida una ilusión marina
> de un pescador que un día ya no puede pescar".

The last of the "Parábolas" [viii] is more successful, though too long to quote in full. Here, the fishing imagery is only implied in the last lines : in the rest of the poem, it is the bee, not the fish, which represents life in time. What makes this poem particularly striking is the way in which the conflict between reason and intuition is made to take place within the poet himself. Two voices, in fact, are speaking : that of the intuitive Machado (stanzas 1 and 2) and that of his rational *alter ego* (stanzas 3 and 4). In the second stanza, the first voice accuses the other :

> Echaste un velo de sombra
> sobre el bello mundo, y vas
> creyendo ver, porque mides
> la sombra con un compás.

The analytical mind, in other words, only thinks it grasps reality; in actual fact, it simply measures shadows of its own making. In the rest of the poem, it admits as much : it has no means of coming to terms with the changing activity of the bee which, like the fish in the other poem, moves in the real world of time. Instead, it is condemned to move in a vicious circle in which successive degrees of abstraction – percept, concept, idea – merely force it back to the starting-point.

In so far as these arguments relate to poetry in general, Machado's position can be stated quite briefly. If logical discourse implies abstraction, its main purpose is to relate one object to another, so that the emphasis falls on what they have in common, rather than on what makes them separate. Poetry, on the other hand, tries to capture the sense of the individuality of things, or the uniqueness of a particular experience. Yet, for all this, philosophy has its uses for the poet, provided he continues to think as a poet. Machado's admiration for Kant, for instance, comes from the sense that, by demonstrating the errors of earlier philosophers, he has made it possible to construct a new theory of knowledge which will correspond more closely to objective reality. Very little of this is made explicit at the time of *Campos de Castilla* : the closest Machado comes to such a claim is in no. xxxix of "Proverbios y cantares", which describes, somewhat flippantly, Kant's critique of reason. What he is saying here, roughly, is that the bird of reason, though sadly diminished after Kant's critical attentions, is once again attempting to fly, to the best of its limited powers. Its flight would be in the direction of Plato, for Machado the supreme example of reason in the service of society, and the essential source of any theory of knowledge. And if this is true, Machado clearly approves, though the situation is presented as hearsay and the final applause is a little disbelieving.*

Whether Machado's prediction was right scarcely matters, though some critics have attempted to relate his line of thought to the phenomenology of the 1920s.† What impresses one is his sensitivity to a changing situation, and the fact that he was prepared to entertain such views for what he felt them to be worth. Some of his liveliest reflections on philosophy, both in the Baeza period and later, come from his realization that there are certain philosophers who themselves are critical of traditional philosophical methods. One of these is Unamuno; another is Bergson, whose name inevitably occurs in discussions of certain poems written between 1912 and 1917. As Nigel Glendinning has shown in an excellent article (*21*), the effect of Bergson on Machado's verse is confined to less than a dozen poems, not all of which were included in the second version of *Campos de Castilla*. Nevertheless, his influence, though less than some critics have tended to suppose, is undeniable, and has a good deal to do with the way Machado sees the conflict between poetry

---

*Compare the following passage from *Reflexiones sobre la lírica* (1925): "En el camino hacia abajo del intelectualismo está Bergson, quizás, en el límite. Para refutarle, habrá que volver de algún modo a Platón, a afirmar nuevamente la posición teórica del pensar; porque la inteligencia pragmática no sirve para el caso" (*4*, II, 125).

†For example, José María Valverde, *5*, 58–9.

and reason. Up to a point, the parallel is close: for Bergson, as for Machado, the intellect can only provide abstract systems of analysis; it is unable to deal with the complexities of the poetic imagination. This is one of the basic arguments of the *Essai sur les données immédiates de la conscience* (1889), to which Machado refers specifically in "Poema de un día". The real task of philosophy, according to Bergson, is to return to the "immediate data of consciousness" – i.e. what takes place in the mind before conceptualization – and to describe these without destroying the organic nature of experience. The essence of consciousness, he argues, is duration ("durée"): time, change, separateness and continuity. To grasp this demands a special kind of reflection, the "thinking in duration" which he calls intuition. Though he is critical of other aspects of Bergson's philosophy, what attracts Machado, clearly, is the relationship he establishes between consciousness, intuition and time, and the possibility of a kind of knowledge which does not depend on intellectual analysis. Nevertheless, it is wrong to imagine that, whenever he writes of time, Machado is thinking on Bergsonian lines. As Glendinning rightly points out:

> . . . only the idea of things *in* time, as opposed to subject to it, is truly Bergsonian, and there are relatively few of Machado's poems which deal with this aspect of time in plainly philosophical terms (*21*, 51).

Two of these – no. xxxv of "Proverbios y cantares" and the eighth of the "Parábolas" – I have already discussed: in both poems, the terms which express the conflict between intuition and reason and the notion of creatures moving in time leave no doubt as to their source. In other poems, it is harder to be certain: the influence of Unamuno – himself an admirer of Bergson – sometimes overlaps to such an extent that it is difficult to tell one version of anti-intellectualism from the other.

Both Unamuno and Bergson figure – along with a great deal else – in one of Machado's most impressive poems, "Poema de un día: meditaciones rurales" [CXXVIII]. This seems a good poem to end on, since, apart from its quality, it draws together a great many of the different strands which run through the poetry of

the Baeza period. As the sub-title suggests, it is a series of medi-
tations which have their source in the poet's actual surroundings.
Yet, though the poem is basically a soliloquy, there is one point
at which Machado directly addresses Unamuno, and there are
other passages which appear to have been written with Unamuno
in mind. The structure is deceptively simple: the "day" of the
poem begins in the afternoon and ends at night, and in the
course of this time, the poet moves from his room to a local
tertulia and back again. In a sense, the whole effect of the poem
depends on casual associations, yet the result is anything but
rambling. This comes about, partly because of the way in which
the chance happenings of an ordinary day are shaped by the
poet's thoughts, and partly through certain recurring images to
which these give rise.

The unifying theme of the poem is time: not in the specifically Bergsonian meaning of flux, but, quite simply, in the sense
of "time passing". The opening lines establish the speaker in a
particular time and place, and also mark out a temporal division
in his own life. ("Yesterday I was a poet of sorts; now I am
merely a teacher of languages.") Like "En estos campos de la
tierra mía . . .", this is a poem written out of a sense of mental
and emotional sterility, though here the feeling of alienation is
concentrated almost entirely on the present. As the meditation
develops, it tends to revolve around two opposing effects of time:
decay and growth. In the first few stanzas, Machado thinks in-
intermittently of the labourers in the fields. For them, he reflects,
the rain is a promise of harvest; he himself is a "fantástico labrador", a "tiller of the imagination", a phrase which establishes
a sense of fellow-feeling and at the same time suggests the very
different, though equally exposed, task of the poet. Later, the
phrase is repeated: "Fantástico labrador,/vuelvo a mis campos."
It would be possible to read this metaphorically: "I return to *my*
fields, the fields of the imagination." Yet this, surely, is wrong.
Machado's mind has temporarily wandered from the fields of
the opening stanzas, so that in effect he is saying: "Vuelvo a mi
tema: los campos." What follows, indeed, refers to the real
fields, though the mood is not quite the same as before. What
has changed it is the presence of the intervening stanza ("En mi

estancia, iluminada . . . la muerte se lo llevó."). Here, Machado's attention is concentrated on one thing: the ticking of the clock in his room, the "corazón de metal" whose monotony seems to echo the tedium of his surroundings. The force of the passage depends on the recognition that there are two sorts of time, the time of the clock, and the more inward sense of time which comes from one's own experience. This, for Machado, is the only "real" time, and inevitably it brings with it thoughts of death:

> Pero ¿tu hora es la mía?
> ¿Tu tiempo, reloj, el mío?
> (Tic-tic, tic-tic . . .) Era un día
> (tic-tic, tic-tic . . .) que pasó,
> y lo que yo más quería
> la muerte se lo llevó.

Though the change to the next stanza is clearly marked – the sound of bells recalls the speaker to the world outside his room –, the idea of death persists through the lines on the rain. These lines, far from being "divagatorios y confusos", as Sánchez Barbudo calls them (*13*, 274), create a mood which is subtly different from that of the opening stanza. This is not just a matter of the presence of death, but of the way death is made to lead back to thoughts of life. Machado achieves this with great skill, through a pair of discreet literary allusions. The lines

> Señor, ¿no es tu lluvia ley
> en los campos que ara el buey
> y en los palacios del rey?

seem a conscious echo of Horace's famous statement: "pallida Mors aequo pulsat pede pauperum tabernas/regumque turres" ("Pale death tramples with equal foot the huts of the poor and the towers of kings") (*Odes* I, iv). At the same time, Machado twists the allusion so that it refers, not to death, but to the life-giving rain, so that in a sense life and death are held in balance within the single sentence. And something similar happens in the next few lines; behind the image of the water which runs into the sea are the well-known verses from the *Coplas* of Jorge Manrique:

> Nuestras vidas son los ríos
> que van a dar en la mar
> que es el morir . . .

In Machado's lines, it is not life which moves towards the sea, but the rain which is a source of life, though the comparison itself – "como este tiempo de hastío" – implies sterility, if not actual death. Yet, if we read the passage with the *Coplas* in mind, the effect is very striking: at the very moment when we expect a reference to death ("corriendo a la mar remota"), the sense appears to swerve in the opposite direction: ". . . con cuanto quiere *nacer*" (my italics). "Appears to", that is, since the effect is not strictly logical; the basic structure of the passage is: "Agua buena, . . . que vas corriendo a la mar remota, . . . sé piadosa . . . con cuanto quiere nacer." Yet the presence of the word "nacer" at this point, however fortuitous, is curiously in keeping with the rest of the passage, which is half-elegy, half-celebration. And the surge of the last lines brings with it a similar balancing of hope and frustration: the rain is now a promise of fresh life in a human, as well as a natural, sense ("carne rosa"), yet it is as if the poet could not rise to the mood of belief which his own excitement has helped to generate.

The final exclamation, with its coupling of "razón" and "locura", may suggest Unamuno, whose presence is never far from the rest of the poem. The transition to the next stanza is not as abrupt as it seems: in retrospect, the thoughts of national revival – "esta España que se agita/porque nace o resucita" – seem to arise naturally from the fertility images of the previous passage. The book of Unamuno's to which Machado refers is presumably *Del sentimiento trágico de la vida*, published in the same year as the poem. In endorsing Unamuno's "philosophy", he is clearly thinking of its anti-rational aspects, though there may be other echoes of Unamuno at this point. Thus, as Ribbans has pointed out (*12*, 310), the phrase "Agua del buen manantial" recalls a sentence in one of Unamuno's earlier letters:

> Recorra, pues, la virgen selva española, y rasgue su costra y busque debajo de la sobrehaz calicostrada el agua que allí corre, agua del manantial soterraño.

Another of the things which help to bind the poem together is the quantity of references to water: rain, springs, rivers and sea. Here, of course, the water is poetry itself, defined in terms which Unamuno would surely have approved:

> Agua del buen manantial,
> siempre viva,
> fugitiva;
> poesía, cosa cordial.

True poetry, then, both "comes from the heart" – a belief which Machado expresses in many forms in the course of his writing – and is constantly in movement, like the water it resembles. And, though the juxtaposition is apparently casual, there is a certain appropriateness in the mention of Bergson, whose philosophy also hinges on the concept of flux. What Machado goes on to say is partly critical:

> Este Bergson es un tuno;
> ¿verdad, maestro Unamuno?
> Bergson no da como aquel
> Immanuel
> el volatín inmortal;
> este endiablado judío
> ha hallado el libre albedrío
> dentro de su mechinal.

The tone of mockery – good-humoured rather than otherwise – conceals a serious point: Bergson, for all his concern with free-will, has nothing to say on the question of God or immortality. Kant, on the other hand, denies the rational proofs of God, but goes on to postulate a God who is "known" only by faith. It is this "leap into faith" – the "volatín inmortal" – which Machado is contrasting with Bergson's agnosticism. And, though he does not say so explicitly, he is aware that Unamuno himself is intensely concerned with the problem of free-will, and that he sees it largely as a question of the nature of man's dependence on his creator. Machado's attitude to Bergson here is half-sceptical, half-admiring: the question of free-will *is* important, he seems to imply, and there is something to be said for both Bergson and Kant. Yet is it all that important, compared with the fact of death, about which philosophers tend to be silent?

The argument, such as it is, trails off as Machado reflects on the vanity of all speculation. The skill of the poem at this point lies in the way the feeling of mental frustration is linked with his surroundings:

> ¡Oh, estos pueblos! Reflexiones,
> lecturas y acotaciones
> pronto dan en lo que son:
> bostezos de Salomón.

The stanza which follows, though it is one of the great triumphs of the poem, hardly needs any comment. In a sense, it is a perfect dramatization of the Baeza which Machado describes in his letter to Unamuno (see above, pp. 65–6), the "páramo espiritual... [donde] no se puede escribir nada suave, porque necesita uno la indignación para no helarse también". The hollow emphases of the conversation ("– Yo no sé,/Don José . . .") are beautifully caught, and the clichés of small-town politics are woven unerringly into the rhythms of the verse. At the same time, this is much more than simple reporting: in its own way, the conversation in the *tertulia* is made to reflect the central theme of the poem:

> Todo llega y todo pasa.
> Nada eterno:
> ni gobierno
> que perdure,
> ni mal que cien años dure.

Surely, but unobtrusively, the whole episode is brought round to certain basic images: the rain and the people in the fields. The poem ends, as it began, in the poet's room, with the ticking of the clock and the copy of Bergson on the table. The final reflection is a philosophical one:

> Sobre mi mesa *Los datos*
> *de la conciencia*, inmediatos.
> No está mal
> este yo fundamental,
> contingente y libre, a ratos,
> creativo, original;
> este yo que vive y siente

> dentro la carne mortal
> ¡ay! por saltar impaciente
> las bardas de su corral.*

Again, Machado approves of Bergson, but only up to a point:
Bergson's idea of a "moi fondamental" – the organic, intuitive
self, which is free to initiate its own process of growth – "no está
mal". Yet, ultimately, Bergson's notions of freedom are unsatis-
factory: the "creation of ourselves by ourselves" is after all a
kind of determination, so that, in a sense, the attempt to define
freedom in Bergsonian terms tends to do away with the idea of
freedom itself. Machado, of course, is not as specific as this,
though his use of Bergson's own vocabulary suggests that he was
aware of the problem. His basic objection, however, is that such
a theory, though attractive in so far as it stresses intuition, allows
no room for the possibility of immortality. This is the point
which he made earlier in the poem: there, free-will was simply
a product of Bergson's own mind ("ha hallado el libre albedrío/
dentro de su mechinal"); here, the "yo que vive y siente" is a
prisoner of the body. Or so Machado imagines: in the last four
lines of the poem he appears to move away from Bergson and to
return to his own speculations. It is hard to be sure of this. As
Glendinning has noticed, there is a certain ambiguity at this
point: is Machado referring to the desire of the "yo fundamen-
tal" to achieve complete liberty? Or is he – as seems more likely
– thinking of the soul's wish to break free of the body at death?
Perhaps, as Glendinning suggests, the ambiguity is intentional,
"since the whole poem maintains a tension between optimistic
and pessimistic views of time and man's freedom of action" (21,
67, n. 1). And this, surely, is the real achievement of the poem:
in the end, what matters more than any specific debts to Bergson
is the fact that Machado has used such ideas as stepping-stones
in following out his more personal meditation. The sense of time
which colours the whole poem is his own, not Bergson's, and it
arises, not merely from abstract thinking, but from the patient
observation of things and people.

*This is a favourite metaphor of Machado's. See his letter to Unamuno
of 1904: "Yo, al menos, sería un ingrato si no reconociera que a usted debo
el haber saltado la tapia de mi corral" (quoted 7, 26). Also "Proverbios
y cantares", no. xxxix: "dicen que quiere saltar / las tapias del corralón".

7 Conclusion

Though "Poema de un día" is one of the earliest of the Baeza poems, it shows more clearly than any other the range and character of Machado's poetry at this period. Taken as a whole, *Campos de Castilla* is a collection of extraordinary variety, with a high proportion of successes, at least half-a-dozen of which are among the finest modern poems in the language. At the same time, its variety is in no way arbitrary: very few of Machado's poems are occasional pieces, and it would be hard to mistake his verse for anyone else's. Literary critics are perhaps too prone to speak of a poet's "development". Where Machado is concerned, one is aware, not of any outstripping of earlier selves, but of a core of integrity which can be recognized at every stage in his work. It is this which ensures the consistency with which he is able to assimilate a great many kinds of experience and which keeps the balance between the personal and the social. As Machado himself realized, to keep such a balance is never easy, least of all when one is writing in a consciously subjective tradition. This explains why, at several points in his career, he appears quite deliberately to change direction. The obvious example of this is the search for greater "objectivity" which begins after *Soledades*. Yet this only partly accounts for the differences between the early poems and *Campos de Castilla*, which, paradoxically, contains some of his finest personal poems. As I have tried to show, there are differences, but there is also continuity, the continuity of a temperament which remains clear-sighted even at moments of doubt and personal crisis. For Machado, as for any serious poet, the writing of poems involves constant reflection on the possibilities of poetry itself. Certainly no other modern Spanish poet has thought so persistently, or so intelligently, about such possibilities, even at the risk of undermining his own art. As José María Valverde has written:

. . . la trayectoria de la obra y la experiencia espiritual de Antonio Machado constituyen un intento de superar el individualismo romántico, tras de apurarlo hasta el fondo, al principio abriéndolo hacia el mundo objetivo – el paisaje de Castilla –, para reconocerse luego personalmente fracasado – "lo Otro" resulta ser "lo Uno", aunque engañosamente disfrazado de objetividad –, pero dejando abierta la esperanza de otras edades históricas en que el hombre vuelva a tener conciencia de la realidad de los demás hombres, incluso como la base de la renovación de la fe religiosa (5, 11).

As a summary, this is admirable, though only a knowledge of the whole work can confirm its accuracy. And this, perhaps, is the essential point : *Campos de Castilla*, though it exists in its own right as an accomplished and memorable collection, points forward as well as back. Already in certain poems of the Baeza period one can sense the direction which Machado's work was to take after 1917. What this amounts to is an admission that he can no longer say all that he has to say in the form of poems, and that to some extent the manner of his earlier poems is no longer possible. Hence the invented figures of the "apocryphal" writings, *Juan de Mairena*, *Abel Martín* and *Los complementarios* : masks through which Machado can speak freely precisely because of the ironical distance which allows him to conceal his own point of view. Critics who refer to the decline in Machado's poetic powers after *Campos de Castilla* take too narrow a view of poetry, as he himself would have been the first to observe. It would be truer to say that, for part of his life, Machado was exclusively a poet and that later he became a writer in both prose and verse, whose prose, more often than not, was a direct consequence of his concerns as a poet. Few poets have been so consistent with themselves as to invent what amounts to a new literary genre; most would be content to have written a *Campos de Castilla*, though this in itself would hardly have been possible without the insight and the intelligence which make the rest of the work seem so inevitable.*

---

*I am indebted to Professor Geoffrey Ribbans for his helpful comments on this study.

Appendix

Poems included in first edition of Campos de Castilla (*1912*).
The numbers are those of the collected poems. The book was divided into five sections, as follows:

I [*Campos de Castilla*]
   Retrato [XCVII]; A orillas del Duero [XCVIII]; Por tierras de España [XCIX]; El hospicio [C]; Fantasía iconográfica [CVII]; Un criminal [CVIII]; Amanecer de otoño [CIX]; Noche de verano [CXI]; Pascua de resurrección [CXII]; Campos de Soria [CXIII].
II La tierra de Alvargonzález [CXIV].
III Proverbios y cantares [CXXXVI, i-xxvi; li-lii].
IV [*Humoradas*]
   En tren [CX] (lines 23–49 only); Consejos [CXXXVII, iv]; Profesión de fe [CXXXVII, v]; Mi bufón [CXXXVIII].
V [*Elogios*]
   A Don Miguel de Unamuno [CLI]; A Juan Ramón Jiménez [CLII].

Bibliographical Note

EDITIONS

1. Albornoz, Aurora de and Torre, Guillermo de (ed.). Antonio Machado, *Obras: poesía y prosa*. Buenos Aires, 1964. The most comprehensive one-volume edition, with bibliography; unfortunately out of print at time of writing.
2. Macrí, Oreste (ed.). Antonio Machado, *Poesie*. 3rd ed., Milan, 1969. The most scholarly edition of the poems, with excellent bibliography. Introduction and notes are in Italian.
2a. Ferreres, Rafael (ed.). Antonio Machado, *Campos de Castilla*. Temas de España, Taurus, Madrid, 1970. Good cheap edition, with useful notes.
3. Torre, Guillermo de (ed.). Antonio Machado, *Los complementarios*. Buenos Aires, 1957. Includes Machado's letters to Unamuno.
4. Albornoz, Aurora de (ed.). Antonio Machado, *Antología de su prosa* (4 vols). I: *Cultura y sociedad;* II: *Literatura y arte;* III: *Decires y pensares filosóficos;* IV: *A la altura de las circunstancias.* Madrid, 1970–71. The best introduction to the prose; comprehensive and well-edited.
5. Valverde, José María (ed.). Antonio Machado, *Nuevas canciones y De un cancionero apócrifo*. Clásicos Castalia, Madrid, 1971. Though strictly an edition of Machado's later poems, the long introduction contains intelligent comments on *Campos de Castilla* and on Machado's work as a whole. (Ricardo Gullón is preparing an edition of *Soledades, galerías y otros poemas* and *Campos de Castilla* for the same series.)
6. Tomlinson, Charles and Gifford, Henry. *Castilian ilexes: versions from Antonio Machado*. London, 1963. Excellent verse translations, with a short but perceptive introduction.

BOOKS

7. Albornoz, Aurora de. *La presencia de Miguel de Unamuno en Antonio Machado*. Madrid, 1968. A thorough examination of the relationship between Machado and Unamuno, with many comments on individual poems.
8. Blanco Aguinaga, Carlos. *Juventud del 98*. Madrid, 1970. A study of the early political affiliations of the 1898 writers, with an interesting final section on Machado.
9. Cernuda, Luis. *Estudios sobre poesía española contemporánea*. Madrid, 1957. Contains chapters on *modernismo*, Unamuno and Machado. Highly personal and at times unfair, but full of interesting observations.
10. Gullón, Ricardo. *Una poética para Antonio Machado*. Madrid, 1970. More concerned with the theoretical implications of Machado's poetics, but also refers to a number of individual poems.
11. Gutiérrez-Girardot, Rafael. *Poesía y prosa en Antonio Machado*. Madrid, 1969. Rather abstrusely written, but at times very perceptive.
12. Ribbans, Geoffrey. *Niebla y soledad: aspectos de Unamuno y Machado*. Madrid, 1972. The definitive study of the early poems; essential for understanding the transition to *Campos de Castilla*.

13. Sánchez Barbudo, Antonio. *Los poemas de Antonio Machado*. Barcelona, 1967. A poem by poem analysis of the entire work. Tends to over-emphasize content, but extremely useful, even when one disagrees with the interpretations.

14. Tuñón de Lara, Manuel. *Antonio Machado, poeta del pueblo*. Barcelona, 1967. The fullest biography so far; by no means definitive, but very readable.

15. Zubiría, Ramón de. *La poesía de Antonio Machado*. Madrid, 1955. A pioneering work in many ways; the chapters on imagery are still essential reading.

ARTICLES

Some of the best articles have appeared in the special Machado numbers of certain critical journals, the two most important of which are *Cuadernos Hispanoamericanos*, XI–XII (1949) and *La Torre*, XII, 45–6 (1964). (The latter also contains a very thorough bibliography.) Of the many articles and essays which refer to specific poems or aspects of *Campos de Castilla*, the following are among the most useful:

16. Alonso, Dámaso. "Fanales de Antonio Machado", in *Cuatro poetas españoles* (Madrid, 1962), 137–78.

17. Beceiro, Carlos. "El poema a José María Palacio de Antonio Machado", *Insula*, XII, 137 (1958), 5.

18. Beceiro, Carlos. "Sobre la fecha y las circunstancias del poema *A José María Palacio*", *La Torre*, XII, 45–6 (1964), 39–57.

19. Blanco Aguinaga, Carlos. "Sobre la 'autenticidad' de la poesía de Antonio Machado", *La Torre*, XII, 45–6 (1964), 387–408.

20. Gaos, Vicente. "En torno a un poema de Antonio Machado [*A José María Palacio*]", in *Claves de literatura española*, Vol. II (Madrid, 1971), 57–80.

21. Glendinning, Nigel. "The philosophy of Henri Bergson in the poetry of Antonio Machado", *Revue de Littérature Comparée*, XXXVI (1962), 50–70.

22. Grant, Helen. " 'Angulos de enfoque' en la poesía de Antonio Machado ", *La Torre*, XII, 45–6 (1964), 455–81.

23. Grant, Helen. "Antonio Machado and *La tierra de Alvargonzález*", *Atlante*, II (1954), 139–58.

24. Grant, Helen. "Apostillas a una edición de 1917 de las *Poesías completas* de Antonio Machado", *Insula*, XIV, 158 (1960), 7.

25. Phillips, Allen. "*La tierra de Alvargonzález*: verso y prosa", *Nueva Revista de Filología Hispánica*, IX (1955), 129–48.

26. Predmore, Richard L. "El tiempo en la poesía de Antonio Machado", *Publications of the Modern Language Association of America*, LXIII (1948), 696–711.

27. Zardoya, Concha. "Los caminos de Antonio Machado", *La Torre*, XII, 45–6 (1964), 75–98.